ISSUES THAT CONCERN YOU

Homosexuality

Tamara L. Roleff, *Book Editor*

GREENHAVEN PRESS
A part of Gale, Cengage Learning

GALE
CENGAGE Learning™

Detroit • New York • San Francisco • New Haven, Conn • Waterville, Maine • London

Elizabeth Des Chenes, *Managing Editor*

© 2012 Greenhaven Press, a part of Gale, Cengage Learning

Gale and Greenhaven Press are registered trademarks used herein under license.

For more information, contact:
Greenhaven Press
27500 Drake Rd.
Farmington Hills, MI 48331-3535
Or you can visit our Internet site at gale.cengage.com

For product information and technology assistance, contact us at

Gale Customer Support, 1-800-877-4253
For permission to use material from this text or product, submit all requests online at www.cengage.com/permissions

Further permissions questions can be e-mailed to permissionrequest@cengage.com

Articles in Greenhaven Press anthologies are often edited for length to meet page requirements. In addition, original titles of these works are changed to clearly present the main thesis and to explicitly indicate the author's opinion. Every effort is made to ensure that Greenhaven Press accurately reflects the original intent of the authors. Every effort has been made to trace the owners of copyrighted material.

Cover image Rikke/Shutterstock.com

LIBRARY OF CONGRESS CATALOGING-IN-PUBLICATION DATA

Homosexuality / Tamara L. Roleff, book editor.
   p. cm. -- (Issues that concern you)
 Includes bibliographical references and index.
 ISBN 978-0-7377-5904-4 (hardcover : alk. paper)
 1. Homosexuality--United States. 2. Homosexuality--Religious aspects--Christianity.
 3. Gay military personnel--Government policy--United States. I. Roleff, Tamara L., 1959-
 HQ76.3.U5H6445 2011
 306.76'60973--dc23
                                         2011023758

Printed in the United States of America
1 2 3 4 5 6 7 15 14 13 12 11

CONTENTS

Introduction   5

1. **The Bible Says That Homosexuality Is a Sin**   10
   Mike Ratliff

2. **Citing the Bible to Condemn Homosexuality Is Hypocritical**   16
   Jon Meacham

3. **Homosexuals Are Not Born Gay**   20
   Peter Sprigg

4. **Homosexuality Most Likely Results from a Combination of Genes and Environment**   26
   Barry Starr

5. **Homosexual Attractions Can Be Changed**   32
   Jason Park

6. **There Is No Evidence That Sexual Orientation Can Be Changed**   40
   Wayne Besen

7. **Same-Sex Marriage Would Undermine the Institution of Marriage**   44
   Witherspoon Institute

8. **Same-Sex Marriage Does Not Harm Heterosexual Marriage**   51
   Theodore B. Olson

9. **Civil Unions Are a Reasonable Alternative to Same-Sex Marriage**   61
   David Blankenhorn and Jonathan Rauch

10. Civil Unions Make Homosexuals
    Second-Class Citizens   67
    Douglas Sharp

11. The Repeal of "Don't Ask, Don't Tell" Will Have
    Little Impact on the US Military   74
    Carter F. Ham and Jeh Charles Johnson

12. "Don't Ask, Don't Tell" Should Not Be Repealed   83
    John McCain

Appendix

    What You Should Know About Homosexuality   88
    What You Should Do About Homosexuality   91

Organizations to Contact   96

Bibliography   103

Index   107

Picture Credits   112

In March 2006 Marine Lance Corporal Matthew Snyder was killed in a vehicle accident in Al Anbar Province in Iraq. When family and friends gathered for his funeral in Westminster, Massachusetts, seven members of Westboro Baptist Church, a small church based in Topeka, Kansas, were also in attendance. They did not come to extend their sympathy to the family, however; they came to protest what they see as national support for homosexuality. The members of Westboro Baptist Church believe that the deaths of American troops fighting in Iraq and Afghanistan are God's punishment for society's tolerance and support of homosexuality. It makes no difference to members of the church whether or not the soldiers are gay (Snyder was not). Holding signs such as "God Hates Fags," "AIDS Cures Fags," and "Thank God for Dead Soldiers," the church members protest at military funerals, high school plays, and other events that are likely to generate publicity. According to press releases put out by Westboro Baptist Church, its members believe "It's NOT OK to be gay. It will damn the soul, destroy the life, and doom any nation that tolerates such evil. God Hates Fags is a profound theological statement, which America needs more than it needs oxygen or bread."[1]

While the Westboro Baptist Church's beliefs about homosexuality are extreme, as are its methods of generating publicity, its views about the immorality of homosexuality are shared by various other religious denominations, pro-family organizations, and individuals, most of whom tend to hold conservative views. Conservative organizations teach their followers that homosexuality is abnormal, unnatural, and considered an abomination by God. In addition, a few—like the members of Westboro Baptist Church—believe that many of society's ills, ranging from high rates of divorce, abortion, mental illness, and sexually transmitted diseases to the AIDS epidemic, drug abuse and sexual promiscuity, are due to the homosexual lifestyle. Furthermore, many believe that homosexuals are trying to impose their so-called gay values of promiscuity and immorality on society, including children.

Conservatives and some religious denominations also actively oppose the "gay agenda," which they define as forcing society to become more tolerant of homosexuality by teaching schoolchil-

Members of the Westboro Baptist Church demonstrate in Baltimore, Maryland. Although the church's antigay position is considered extreme by critics, many religious denominations share their views on homosexuality.

dren about notable achievements of homosexuals; passing laws prohibiting discrimination against gays; designating violence targeted toward gays as a hate crime; permitting gays to openly serve in the military; and changing the definition of marriage to allow same-sex couples to wed. Another fear opponents have is that if items from this so-called gay agenda are legalized, children will be forced to learn about homosexuality in school as early as in kindergarten. Not only do these conservative parents want to shield their young children from the sexual details of homosexuality, but they are also concerned that their children will become desensitized to homosexuality and therefore more tolerant and accepting of what they consider a deviant and immoral lifestyle.

One aspect of this lifestyle—gay marriage—has become a prominent and polarizing issue during the last few years. Opponents of gay marriage argue that marriage is a religious sacrament. They also argue that the needs of children can be best met in a household in which there is a father and a mother, not two parents of the same gender. Cary Gordon, pastor of the Cornerstone World Outreach Church in Sioux City, Iowa, spoke at a rally protesting same-sex marriage, saying, "There are natural laws that men did not make and we don't have the power to overrule. One of those laws is it takes one man and one woman to make a baby. . . . That is the logical definition of family." He added that a same-sex couple could never raise a child as well as a heterosexual couple can. "When two men say to the world we can raise a child just as good as any heterosexual couple, I think that's offensive to women, because you're saying that a woman, a female, does not bring a unique contribution."[2]

More liberal religious denominations and individuals tend to believe that homosexuality is set at birth, is unchangeable, and is a natural and normal behavior, albeit for a small minority of people. They consider the issues associated with homosexuality—gay marriage and parenting, discrimination, and gays in the military, for example—as civil rights issues. Many civil rights organizations such as the American Civil Liberties Union, Human Rights Campaign, and the Gay and Lesbian Alliance Against Defamation are working to extend to gays the civil rights that heterosexuals take for granted: the rights to marry; to adopt children; to be free from discrimination in their employment and housing; and to openly serve in the military.

The courts are gradually beginning to agree that gays are being discriminated against in these areas. In recent years courts at many levels have overturned laws and constitutional amendments that banned same-sex marriage and permitted discrimination in the workplace and in housing. Furthermore, in December 2010 the US Congress voted to repeal the "don't ask, don't tell" policy that prevented gays from serving openly in the armed forces. Several courts ruled that many of these laws violated the Constitution's Fourteenth Amendment—specifically the equal protection clause, which guarantees all Americans equal protection under the laws. The Reverend Jesse Jackson, in a December 2010 speech about Proposition 8, which banned same-sex marriage in California, urged the court to overturn the state's constitutional amendment.

> We cannot sit idly by while Prop. 8 seeks to target gays and lesbians for a disfavored legal status, as America's newest "second-class citizens." Our legal scholars have cited fourteen times where the Supreme Court has stated that marriage is a fundamental right of all individuals. That principle must be upheld today—for Blacks and Whites, for straight and gay, for ALL Americans. No group of people should be denied their fundamental constitutional liberties, like equal protection under the law, simply because of who they are.[3]

The issues over homosexuality boil down to whether people believe a person's sexual orientation is decided at birth, or whether a person chooses his or her orientation. Many of those who consider homosexuality a lifestyle choice are resisting all attempts to bring gays and lesbians into mainstream society, while supporters of gay rights feel strongly that homosexuals should be accorded the same rights as every other American. The articles in this anthology present a wide range of opinion on the many controversies surrounding homosexuality. In addition, the volume contains appendixes to help the reader understand and explore the topic, including a thorough bibliography and a list of organizations to contact for further information. The appendix titled "What You Should Know About Homosexuality" offers facts about same-sex marriage and other relevant topics. The appendix "What You Should Do About Homosexuality" offers tips for young people struggling to formulate their views or address their own or someone else's sexual orientation issues. With all these features, *Issues That Concern You: Homosexuality* provides a thorough resource for everyone interested in this issue.

Notes

1. Quoted in Anti-Defamation League, "Westboro Baptist Church: In Their Own Words; On Gays." www.adl.org/learn/ext_us/WBC/WBC-on-gays.asp.
2. Quoted in Tyler Kingkade, "High-Profile Pastor: 'Ungodly' Same-Sex Marriage Against 'Natural Law,'" *Iowa Independent*, March 24, 2011. http://iowaindependent.com/54032/gordon-its-not-about-hate-its-about-natural-law.
3. Quoted in Andy Eddings, "Voice for Equality: The Rev. Jesse Jackson," Freedom to Marry, December 8, 2010. www.freedomtomarry.org/blog/entry/voice-for-equality-the-rev.-jesse-jackson.

ONE

The Bible Says That Homosexuality Is a Sin

Mike Ratliff

In the following viewpoint, Mike Ratliff argues that according to God's word as written in the Bible, homosexuality is a sexual perversion and is forbidden by God. Ratliff asserts that it does not matter if the homosexual relations are between two men or two women, it is still an abomination and a sin. Christians must reject compromise and political correctness, he argues, and refuse to accept homosexuality. Ratliff is a Bible teacher and a contributor to the Christian Research Network.

L ast week I found myself watching a special on PBS about the relationships between [former British prime minister] Winston Churchill, FDR [former US president Franklin Delano Roosevelt], and [former Soviet leader] Josef Stalin. Afterwards I did some research into the history of the Communist Party in Soviet Russia. One of the early leaders of the Bolsheviks was Leon Trotsky. After the death of [Russian Communist Party founder Vladimir] Lenin, Trotsky came into conflict with the Bolsheviks, who supported Stalin. He had to leave the country. He wrote articles in hiding that attacked the policies of the Stalinists. One of the "strategies" of Trotsky that was rejected by the Stalinists was

"Continual Revolution." He was a true Communist. According to [Karl] Marx's *Communist Manifesto*, Communism is the goal, but in order to reach it Capitalism must be replaced with Socialism and eventually done away with completely in order to bring in a pure Communistic state. Trotsky was a true believer, while Stalin was more pragmatic. What has this to do with Homosexuality? The "Gay Rights" movement is constructed according to the principles of Leon Trotsky's "Continual Revolution." Its true believers will never stop until they achieve their goal of complete societal acceptance of Homosexuality as a protected minority with all the same legal rights as non-homosexuals, but with the added protection from the Federal and State governments to ensure it.

A Sexual Perversion

There is a huge push in the visible Church right now to "remove the stigma" of homosexuality as a sin. When I hear directly from a pastor like Rick Warren that he has "gay" friends and believes that the Church should not be so "judgmental" and so accept them as fellow members in our churches, I know that he has compromised and is using his own standards of holiness and righteousness instead of those given to us by God, which we have in His Word. Homosexuality is nothing more than a sexual perversion, which is forbidden by God.

You shall not lie with a male as with a woman; it is an abomination. (Leviticus 18:22 ESV [Bible, English Standard Version])

If a man lies with a male as with a woman, both of them have committed an abomination; they shall surely be put to death; their blood is upon them. (Leviticus 20:13 ESV)

Lesbianism

For those who say the Bible doesn't address Lesbianism, Paul does so very well in the following passage:

> Therefore God gave them up in the lusts of their hearts to impurity, to the dishonoring of their bodies among themselves, because they exchanged the truth about God for a

lie and worshiped and served the creature rather than the Creator, who is blessed forever! Amen. For this reason God gave them up to dishonorable passions. For their women exchanged natural relations for those that are contrary to nature; and the men likewise gave up natural relations with women and were consumed with passion for one another, men committing shameless acts with men and receiving in themselves the due penalty for their error. (Romans 1:24–27 ESV)

Homosexuality, whether between women or men, is an abomination to God. The Hebrew word translated in Leviticus 18:22 as abomination is הבעת or הבעות. This word refers to something that is morally disgusting or an abominable idol. God sees idolatry as the righteous see what is perverse. Sex is subject to idolatry just as is money or possessions. With all of the emphasis we have today on sex it most certainly has become an idol to many.

Many who view homosexuality as a sin point to verses in the book of Leviticus in the Bible to support their claim that homosexuality is a sexual perversion forbidden by God.

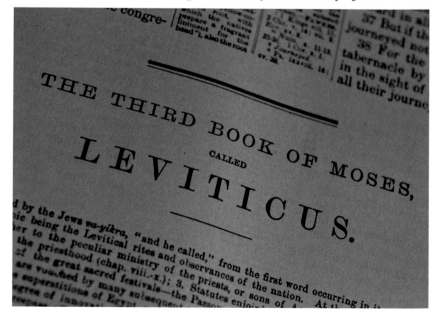

Homosexuality Is a Sin

Homosexuality is a sin. Therefore, men and women can be delivered from it in repentance by God's grace and power. However, we must never forget that there are no exceptions in who will inherit the kingdom of God and who will not. The unrighteous will not, while the righteous will. The unrighteous are marked by sins strictly forbidden by God. On the other hand, those truly in Christ will not be among those who practice these things. Christians are regenerate and are, therefore, new creations. They are not perfect, but they will never be at peace with anything in their lives that carries the stain of unrighteousness. They have a drive to be holy as God is holy.

> Or do you not know that the unrighteous will not inherit the kingdom of God? Do not be deceived: neither the sexually immoral, nor idolaters, nor adulterers, nor men who practice homosexuality, nor thieves, nor the greedy, nor drunkards, nor revilers, nor swindlers will inherit the kingdom of God. (1 Corinthians 6:9–10 ESV)

> Now we know that the law is good, if one uses it lawfully, understanding this, that the law is not laid down for the just but for the lawless and disobedient, for the ungodly and sinners, for the unholy and profane, for those who strike their fathers and mothers, for murderers, the sexually immoral, men who practice homosexuality, enslavers, liars, perjurers, and whatever else is contrary to sound doctrine, in accordance with the gospel of the glory of the blessed God with which I have been entrusted. (1 Timothy 1:8–11 ESV)

Christians Stand Firm Against Sin

Please notice that there are those who profess to be Christians, but who are deceived. These deceived ones attempt to open wide the narrow gate of salvation to include those who are practitioners of the ways of the world. We desperately need men in our pulpits in this day to stand firm on the fact that sin is what cost our Lord Jesus Christ his life. Not His sin, for he was sinless, but the sins of all those for whom He died. How can we continue to

A 2009 telephone survey of more than 9,000 Americans revealed significant differences in the religious beliefs of those who identify themselves as straight and those who consider themselves gay.

Have you made a personal commitment to Jesus Christ that is still important in your life today?

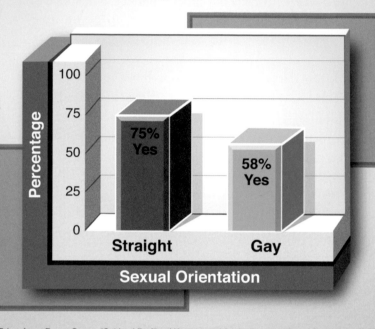

Taken from: Barna Group, "Spiritual Profile of Homosexual Adults Provides Surprising Insights," 2009.

love the sins from which our Lord's shed blood saves us? God's grace is beyond our comprehension, but His Word tells us plainly that even so, Christians are called to be holy, and learn to walk in righteousness.

I overslept this morning so I listened to a different lineup on Bott Radio than I am used to in my drive to work. This morning instead of John MacArthur as I drove in, I listened to "Focus on the Family." Today's broadcast was an interview with [former Miss California and 2009 Miss USA runner-up] Carrie Prejean and her mother. In the part I heard, I distinctly heard her say that she actually has many "gay" friends and has no animosity towards them at all. She contends that those who are all up at arms at what she said about marriage being between a man and a woman are those who are demanding legal rights for men to marry men and women to marry women and have that legally protected just as marriage between men and women. No mention was made of the subsequent issues with her semi-nude pictures and breast augmentation surgery. The main thrust of the discussion was about "tolerance." If those demanding tolerance will not give tolerance to those who disagree then they are simply violating Christ's command to Judge Not! At least, that is the gist of what I heard as I drove through very heavy traffic this morning.

No Compromise

Are we supposed to demand tolerance for our faith from the world or are we supposed to be salt and light in it? Do you see the hypocrisy that creeps into Christians when they compromise with the world? I reject Political Correctness and so should all who take up their crosses and follow the Lord daily in self-denial. Political Correctness is what shapes the vanilla, empty, effeminate institutions in our time that call themselves churches. God is calling His people to stand firm and never compromise no matter how costly it may be. Our preachers must preach the Word no matter how Politically Incorrect it may be. Homosexuality is nothing more than a sexual perversion and we must not compromise on this at all. I would hate to be those Christian leaders who have compromised in their ministries in order to maintain their Political Correctness. They will have to give an account to our Lord when they stand before Him.

TWO

Citing the Bible to Condemn Homosexuality Is Hypocritical

Jon Meacham

In the following viewpoint, Jon Meacham argues that using Bible passages to condemn homosexuality is "the worst kind of fundamentalism." He contends that the usual verses used as biblical authority to attack homosexuals are part of a text that forbids certain haircuts with the same intensity. Meacham therefore believes that condemning homosexuality with the support of Bible passages is hypocritical and that Americans should look at the question of gay marriage anew. Meacham is a former editor of *Newsweek* magazine and a Pulitzer Prize–winning author.

On the campus of Wheaton College in Illinois last Wednesday, in another of the seemingly endless announcements of splintering and schism in the Episcopal Church, the Rt. Rev. Robert Duncan and other leaders of the conservative forces of reaction to the ecclesiastical and cultural acceptance of homosexuality declared that their opposition to the ordination and the marriage of gays was irrevocably rooted in the Bible—which they regard as the "final authority and unchangeable standard for Christian faith and life."

No matter what one thinks about gay rights—for, against or somewhere in between—this conservative resort to biblical authority is the worst kind of fundamentalism. Given the history of the making of the Scriptures and the millennia of critical attention scholars and others have given to the stories and injunctions that come to us in the Hebrew Bible and the Christian New Testament, to argue that something is so because it is in the Bible is more than intellectually bankrupt—it is unserious, and unworthy of the great Judeo-Christian tradition.

As Lisa Miller points out in her cover essay this week, the debate and its implications spread far beyond intramural Anglican conflicts. The impetus for the project came not from Wheaton but from California and the successful passage of Proposition 8, which seeks to ban gay marriage. The issue of marriage (as opposed to civil unions and other middle courses) is not going away: California was a battle in a larger, ongoing war, both in America and in Europe. (For the record, the Lisa Miller who is our religion editor and the author of the cover story is not the Lisa Miller who is featured in Lorraine Ali's companion piece about a gay couple's custody fight.)

Religious Case for Supporting Gay Marriage

Briefly put, the Judeo-Christian religious case for supporting gay marriage begins with the recognition that sexual orientation is not a choice—a matter of behavior—but is as intrinsic to a person's makeup as skin color. The analogy with race is apt, for Christians in particular long cited scriptural authority to justify and perpetuate slavery with the same certitude that some now use to point to certain passages in the Bible to condemn homosexuality and to deny the sacrament of marriage to homosexuals. This argument from Scripture is difficult to take seriously—though many, many people do—since the passages in question are part and parcel of texts that, with equal ferocity, forbid particular haircuts. The Devil, as Shakespeare once noted, can cite Scripture for his purpose, and the texts have been ready sources for those seeking to promote anti-Semitism and limit the human rights of women, among other things that few people in the first decade of the 21st century would think reasonable.

Beyond the Bible, some argue that marriage is between a man and woman by custom and tradition—which is true, but only to a point. As recently as the 1960s men and women of different races could not legally marry in certain states. In civil and reli-

The author argues that for religious conservatives to cite the Bible as the ultimate authority in justifying their antigay agenda is simply foolish and is unworthy of the great Judeo-Christian tradition.

gious terms we have redefined marriage before in order to reflect evolving understandings of justice and right; to act as though marriage has been one thing since Eden (and look how well that turned out) is ahistorical.

In this light it would seem to make sense for Americans to look anew at the underlying issues on the question of gay marriage. One can decide to oppose it in good faith, but such opposition should at least be forged by those in full possession of the relevant cultural and religious history and context. The reaction to this cover is not difficult to predict. Religious conservatives will say that the liberal media are once again seeking to impose their values (or their "agenda," a favorite term to describe the views of those who disagree with you) on a God-fearing nation. Let the letters and e-mails come. History and demographics are on the side of those who favor inclusion over exclusion. (As it has been with reform in America from the Founding forward.) The *Newsweek* Poll confirms what other surveys have also found: that there is a decided generational difference on the issue, with younger people supporting gay marriage at a higher rate than older Americans. One era's accepted reality often becomes the next era's clear wrong. So it was with segregation, and so it will be, I suspect, with the sacrament of marriage.

THREE

Homosexuals Are Not Born Gay

Peter Sprigg

> Peter Sprigg argues in the following viewpoint that being "born gay" is a myth. He discusses studies that found that a very small percentage of identical twins were both gay; if homosexuality is determined by genetics, then identical twins, who share 100 percent of their genes, should both be gay, he asserts. Sprigg is a senior fellow for policy studies at the Family Research Council in Washington, DC, and the coauthor of *Getting It Straight: What the Research Shows About Homosexuality*.

The homosexual activist movement is now over forty years old. Conservatives sometimes refer to the array of goals this movement has pursued—hate crime laws, employment "non-discrimination" laws, same-sex "marriage," etc.—as "the homosexual agenda."

Occasionally, we are mocked for the use of this term, as though we are suggesting that this movement represents some sinister and shadowy conspiracy. However, the term "agenda" is a perfectly neutral one. We in the pro-family movement certainly have our own "agenda." Its elements include: protecting the safety and dignity of human life from the moment of conception to the moment of natural death; encouraging the practice of sexuality only within the context of marriage between one man and one woman; and promoting the natural family, headed by a married, biological mother and father, as the ideal setting for raising children. We are proud of this "agenda," and will continue to vigorously pursue it.

The Homosexual Agenda

By the same token, homosexual activists have a clear agenda as well. It is an agenda that demands the universal acceptance of homosexual acts and relationships—morally, socially, legally, religiously, politically and financially. Indeed, it calls for not only acceptance, but affirmation and celebration of this behavior as normal, natural, and even as desirable for those who desire it. There is nothing shadowy or secretive about this agenda—in fact, it has become nearly impossible to avoid encountering it.

There is at least one key difference between the "pro-family agenda" and the "pro-homosexual agenda." In the case of the pro-family agenda, there is a growing and impressive body of social science research and other evidence confirming that the theoretical foundations of pro-family policies are sound, and that pro-family practices benefit society. New technologies like advanced ultrasound imaging and fetal surgery have confirmed the essential humanity of the unborn. Sexual relations outside of marriage have been shown to lead to an array of negative physical and psychological consequences. And social science research has clearly shown that children who are raised by their own, married, biological mother and father have a significant advantage in a broad range of outcome measures.

The same cannot be said of the homosexual agenda. In large measure, the pursuit of this agenda has involved an effort to define the benefits homosexuals seek as a matter of "civil rights," comparable to that which African Americans fought for in the 1960's; and to define disapproval of homosexual conduct as a form of "bigotry," comparable to a racist ideology of white supremacy.

The Five "I's"

However, these themes only make sense if, in fact, a homosexual "orientation" is a characteristic that is comparable to race. But racial discrimination is not wrong merely because a group of people complained loudly and long that it is wrong. Racial discrimination is irrational and invidious because of what I call the five "I's"—the fact that, as a personal characteristic, race is inborn, involuntary, immutable, innocuous and in the Constitution.

Homosexual activists would have us believe that the same is true of their homosexuality. They want us to believe that their homosexual "orientation" is something they are born with, cannot choose whether to accept or reject, and cannot change; and that it does no harm (to themselves or to society), while being protected by the principles of the Constitution.

However, these are empirical questions, subject to being verified or refuted based on the evidence. And the evidence produced by research has simply not been kind to this theoretical underpinning of the homosexual movement. It has become more and more clear that none of the "five-I" criteria apply to the choice to engage in homosexual conduct.

Myths About Homosexuality

The homosexual movement is built, not on facts or research, but on mythology. Unfortunately, these myths have come to be widely accepted in society—particularly in schools, universities and the media. . . .

[One such myth is that] people are born gay.

[However] the research does not show that anyone is "born gay," and suggests instead that homosexuality results from a complex mix of developmental factors.

The widespread, popular belief that science has proven a biological or genetic origin to homosexuality can be traced to the publicity which surrounded three studies published in the early 1990s. In August of 1991, researcher Simon LeVay published a study based on post-mortem examinations of the brains of cadavers. He concluded that differences in a particular brain structure suggested "that sexual orientation has a biological substrate." In December of 1991, researchers J. Michael Bailey and Richard C. Pillard published a study of identical and fraternal twins and

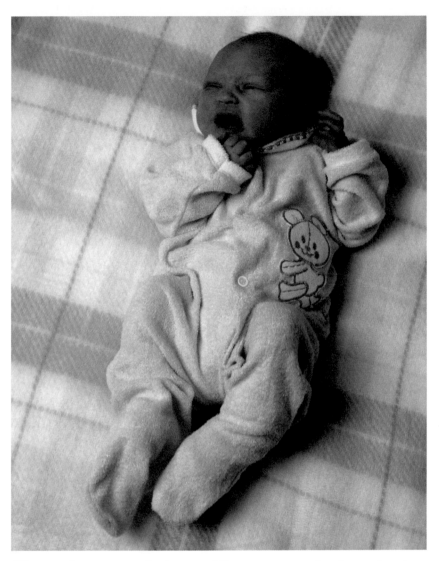

The author contends that, unlike race, sexual orientation is not fixed at birth and that homosexuality occurs as a result of a complex mix of developmental factors.

adoptive brothers, and found that "the pattern of rates of homosexuality . . . was generally consistent with substantial genetic influence." Finally, in 1993, researcher Dean Hamer claimed to have found a specific "chromosomal region" containing "a gene that contributes to homosexual orientation in males."

These studies suffered from serious methodological weaknesses, such as small sample sizes, non-random samples and even possible mis-classification of their subjects. Other scientists have been unable to replicate these dramatic findings. These problems led two psychiatrists to conclude, "Critical review shows the evidence favoring a biologic theory to be lacking. . . . In fact, the current trend may be to underrate the explanatory power of extant psychosocial models."

Studies of Twins

Subsequently, more rigorous studies of identical twin pairs have essentially made it impossible to argue for the genetic determination of homosexuality. Since identical ("monozygotic," in the scientific literature) twins have identical genes, if homosexuality were genetically fixed at birth, we should expect that whenever

Incidence of Same-Sex Romantic Attraction in Both Members of Sibling Pairs

Type of Pair	All		Male		Female	
	Number	%	Number	%	Number	%
Monozygotic twins (identical)	45	6.7	26	7.7	19	5.3
Dizygotic twins (fraternal)	83	7.2	48	4.2	35	11.4
Full siblings	183	5.5	89	4.5	94	6.4
Other	216	4.2	110	2.7	106	5.7
All	527	5.3	273	4.0	254	6.7

Taken from: Peter S. Bearman and Hannah Brückner, "Opposite-Sex Twins and Adolescent Same-Sex Attraction," *American Journal of Sociology*, March 2002.

one twin is homosexual, the other twin would be homosexual (a "concordance rate" of 100%). Even Michael Bailey himself, co-author of the landmark 1991 twins study (which supposedly found a concordance rate of about 50%), conducted a subsequent study on a larger sample of Australian twins. As summarized by other researchers, "They found twenty-seven identical male twin pairs where at least one of the twin brothers was gay, but in only three of the pairs was the second twin brother gay as well" (a "concordance rate" of only eleven percent).

Researchers Peter Bearman and Hannah Brückner, from Columbia and Yale respectively, studied data from the National Longitudinal Study of Adolescent Health, and found even lower concordance rates of only 7.7% for male and 5.3% for female identical twins. In fact, their study neatly refuted several of the biological theories for the origin of homosexuality, finding social experiences in childhood to be far more significant:

> [T]he pattern of concordance (similarity across pairs) of same-sex preference for sibling pairs does not suggest genetic influence independent of social context. Our data falsify the hormone transfer hypothesis by isolating a single condition that eliminates the opposite-sex twin effect we observe—the presence of an older same-sex sibling. We also consider and reject a speculative evolutionary theory that rests on observing birth-order effects on same-sex orientation. In contrast, our results support the hypothesis that less gendered socialization in early childhood and preadolescence shapes subsequent same-sex romantic preferences.

If it was not clear in the 1990's, it certainly is now—no one is "born gay."

FOUR

Homosexuality Most Likely Results from a Combination of Genes and Environment

Barry Starr

> Barry Starr is a geneticist with Stanford University and answers questions in the column Ask a Geneticist on one of the university's websites, The Tech Museum. In the following viewpoint, Starr maintains that both environment and genetics play a role in determining sexuality. He discusses studies of identical twins in which a high percentage of both twins were gay. But, he adds, because identical twins in the study did not share the same sexual orientation 100 percent of the time, the effect of the environment on the brain, perhaps as early as in the womb, must also play a role. He concludes that whatever determines a person's sexuality, it is unlikely that it is a choice.

*I*s homosexuality an inborn, unchangeable part of us or can people actually "convert"? I think it is just the way I am but my classmates and some family members think otherwise. How can I convince them that this really is the way I am supposed to be?

—A high school student from California

Not a Choice

First off, almost all of the data shows that being gay is not a choice. Most people discover they are gay rather than choosing it. As such, it is very difficult to "convert" to heterosexuality. It requires going against who you are.

I have seen no reliable data on the conversion of homosexuals. Or on how well it works, how happy the recently "converted" are, how long they stay "converted", or any other statistics. There is some anecdotal data—things like it worked for me, it can work for you. But nothing that would make it into a scientific journal.

Because of this, I can't evaluate the therapy scientifically. But even proponents say the success rate is pretty low—it doesn't work that often.

One reason why conversion might be so difficult is that the brains of gays may be different from their straight counterparts. For example, a couple of studies have been done that show that the brains of gay people are different than those of straight people. And that gay people respond to pheromones [chemical substances emitted by animals that influence the behavior of others in the species] differently than straight people.

This isn't surprising, sexual attraction resides in the brain. But where do these changes come from? Are they destined by genes, is it something in the environment or a combination of the two?

The best evidence points to the environment and genes both playing a role.

Twin Studies

To try to sort out environment and genes, scientists often do a twin study. In a twin study, identical twins are compared to fraternal twins. If something happens more often in identical twins, then that something is influenced by genes.

How does a twin study show something runs in a family? Remember, identical twins have exactly the same genes. Fraternal twins share only as many genes as any brother or sister.

Because twins are born at the same time, the environment is as same as possible for them. So if something happens more often

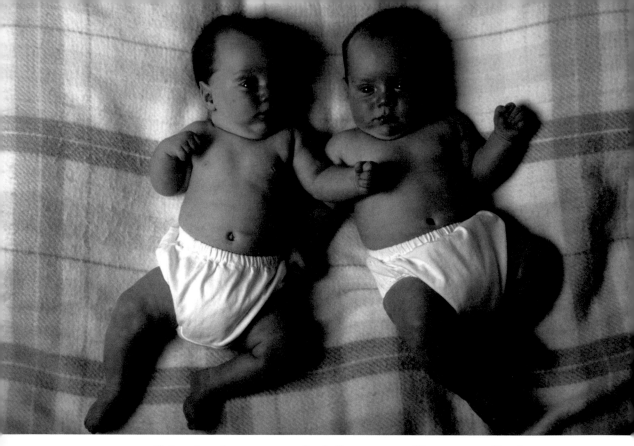

Scientists have researched the causes of homosexuality by studying genetics. Research studies of twins have compared fraternal twins with identical twins to determine whether genetics play a role in sexual orientation.

in identical than in fraternal twins, then it is most likely because they share the same genes.

A number of studies have looked at homosexuality in twins, all with similar results. For example, in one study, if one identical twin was gay, the other was also gay 50% of the time. If they were fraternal twins, they were both gay 22% of the time. And if one was adopted, the chances fell to 11%.

Now these numbers are from one study. Other studies have different percentages but the same trend—identical twins are more likely to both be gay as compared to fraternal twins.

This strongly suggests that there is a genetic component—there is something in their genes that makes them more likely to be gay. Genetics, though, isn't everything. If it were, then identical twins would both be gay 100% of the time. And this clearly isn't the case.

Environmental Effects

And if it were all environment, then identical twins would both be gay as often as fraternal twins. Again, this isn't the situation.

So the interplay of environment and genes probably results in homosexuality. By environment, I don't just mean how someone is raised (although that is sometimes part of it). I mean the effect the environment can have on how the brain is hardwired very early on.

In the womb, things happen that can affect how we develop. A surge of hormones here, a viral infection there, and we are not the same as we would be without these environmental factors.

Handedness is an example of this. Some people have genes that make them more likely to be left-handed. Not all of these folks end up lefties, though.

Something else has to happen while they are developing. Scientists haven't pinpointed what this something is but it is the combination of genes and environment that makes someone left-handed.

Maybe something similar happens with gay people. And since the brain continues to develop after we're born, the environment can affect how our brain develops even after we are born.

The key here, though, is that this all affects how our brains are hardwired. It isn't a choice or something like that, a brain has been configured to be attracted to the same sex.

Evidence

Is there any evidence of this happening? There is some evidence that increased steroids in the womb may increase the chances that a girl will be a lesbian. Some studies show that the more older brothers you have, the more likely it is for you to be gay. Also, gay people tend to be left handed much more often.

The animal evidence is also pretty strong that what happens in the womb can affect the eventual sexual orientation of the fetus. For example, exposure to differing amounts of testosterone or estrogen in the womb can affect whether an animal is hetero- or homosexual.

How would genes work in all of this? What genes would do is either make the fetus more or less sensitive to these hormones or, perhaps, affect how or whether the mother reacts.

So, for example, a surge of hormones may change one fetus' brain but not another's. Or the mother might respond to stress with more hormones causing a change whereas a different mother wouldn't release as much hormone.

Fruit Fly Studies

Whatever the cause, it is very unlikely that just one gene will cause someone to be gay, at least in people. But it is a different story in the fruit fly. . . .

A single DNA mutation can turn a straight male fruit fly into a gay one. A similar mutation in a female fly makes her more interested in the girls than the boys.

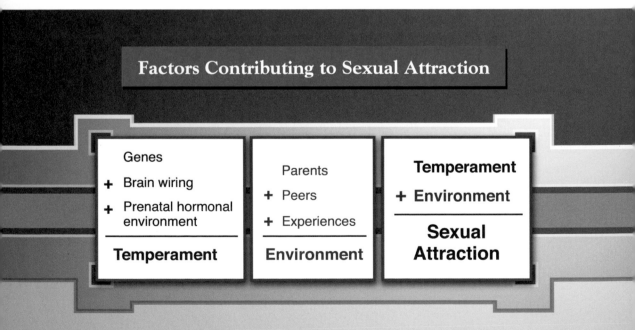

Factors Contributing to Sexual Attraction

Genes
+ Brain wiring
+ Prenatal hormonal environment
———————————
Temperament

Parents
+ Peers
+ Experiences
———————————
Environment

Temperament
+ **Environment**
———————————
Sexual Attraction

Taken from: Julie Harren, "Homosexuality 101: What Every Therapist, Parent, and Homosexual Should Know," National Association for Research and Therapy of Homosexuality, April 9, 2008. www.narth.com/docs/home101.html.

As I said, though, it is pretty unlikely that anything so simple is happening in people. Something so complex most likely involves lots of genes.

Changes in the Brain

So there you have it. Being gay is not being mentally ill (at least according to the American Psychiatric Association). There appear to be real changes in the brain that correlate with being gay. And from the twin studies, it looks like genes play a role.

So can you convert? There isn't any good data on this but most health professionals think that most homosexuals cannot. Whether or not you can convert is really only something you, not your family or friends, can decide.

FIVE

Homosexual Attractions Can Be Changed

Jason Park

The following viewpoint is a first-person account by Jason Park about how he changed his sexual attraction for other men. Park had been experiencing homosexual attractions since puberty and adolescence. When he was in his early thirties and married, Park decided he was tired of leading a double life and that he no longer wanted to have homosexual feelings. He found a therapist who helped him realize that he had been seeking emotional support from men through sexual intimacy. According to Park, once he learned how to develop close platonic friendships with men, his sexual attractions toward men decreased. Park has written three books about helping men change their sexual attraction toward other men.

It has been seventeen years since I resolved my homosexual problems. I use that word purposely. I am not suppressing the feelings. I have filled the underlying needs that created the homosexual attractions, and the problems are resolved. I am happy to say I no longer struggle with homosexuality. It no longer controls my life.

Homosexual Feelings Have Changed

On rare occasions, I still experience a homosexual attraction, but I can dismiss it with minimum effort. It doesn't prevent me from maintaining healthy friendships, marriage, and peace of mind. In the past, when I'd walk by a good-looking man, I would turn around and follow him and undress him in my mind. I would fantasize about how it would be to be in a relationship with him. Within seconds, in my mind, I had moved in to his apartment and for the rest of the day I would be living my life with him in my mind.

Now when I pass the same man on the street, I acknowledge his good looks and leave it at that. It is healthy to notice men and women and be attracted to their good qualities. But I don't fantasize jumping into bed with them. I may admire their good characteristics and have an interest in getting to know them, but as a healthy friendship.

Today I have many good friends and feel fulfilled in male relationships. I feel comfortable with men at work and at my church. I am happy and fulfilled in my marriage and in my roles as husband and father. Through the experiences I have had, I have learned about patience, mercy, and repentance. I have learned a bit about the workings of a loving Heavenly Father in my life. I am a lot less judgmental than I used to be. I've learned that sometimes people have internal struggles that are tremendous, and I admire them for their courage—even though outwardly they may not think they measure up to other people. I don't think I would have learned these lessons had I not had the struggles I've had.

I am at peace.

I want to let people know it is possible to make important changes in their lives. We hear much in the media today saying that if you're gay you're born that way and you can't change it. Some people are happy with that, but there are also many like me who are not happy with it and want something else for their lives. I feel sorry for those who feel they are locked in to it and have no choices. I finally found answers, explored my options, and made informed decisions for myself. . . .

Early Life

My earliest recollection of being attracted toward other males was about age 12. Going through puberty and adolescence, I never labeled myself homosexual; I thought I had normal sexual attractions. However, in retrospect, I can see how they were clearly directed toward males even though I was almost 30 before I admitted to myself that the attractions I experienced were homosexual attractions.

I discovered pornography at about age 15, and was aroused by female pornography. However, my family and church taught me to respect women, and so I felt guilty looking at naked women. When I found a Playgirl magazine, I found it at least as interesting as Playboy, and somehow I didn't feel the same guilt looking at naked men. It seemed more normal, since men saw each other naked in locker rooms. I may also have been more attracted to male than female bodies, because male bodies are inherently more lean than female bodies, and I am attracted to fit, lean bodies. (Even today, I don't know whether I was originally more attracted to male than female pornography, or if I focused on male bodies because I felt less guilty looking at men than women. Then, having focused on it, I'm sure it had some role in shaping my concepts of sexuality.)

I was propositioned at age 16 by a clothing salesman in a dressing room. Although I was intrigued by it, I knew what he was suggesting was wrong, and I had no desire to meet him in the restroom. I left the store quickly. . . .

Coming to Grips with Homosexual Feelings

At age 31, after four years of marriage and three children, I finally admitted I had a homosexual problem and had to determine what to do about it. I thought long and hard about whether this was what I wanted for my life. It didn't fit with being married and having kids—and I wanted my wife and children. It didn't fit with my personal values or my understanding of God's eternal plan for me. If I were going to be married, which I wanted to be, I had to be committed and monogamous. So sexual feelings toward other

The Discrepancy Between Having a Gay Sexual Experience and Identifying as Gay

While about 7 percent of adult women and 8 percent of men identify as gay, lesbian, or bisexual, the proportion of individuals in the United States who have had same-gender sexual interactions at some point in their lives is higher (up to 15 percent for men, 9 percent for women).

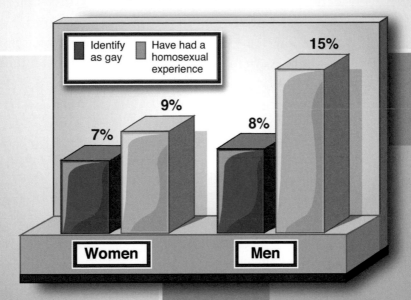

Identify as gay / Have had a homosexual experience

7% 9% 8% 15%

Women   Men

Taken from: National Survey of Health and Behavior, October 2010. www.nationalsexstudy.indiana.edu; Debby Herbenick et al. *Journal of Sexual Medicine*, October 2010. eorder.sheridan.com/3_0/display/index.php?flashpring=726.

men didn't fit. I couldn't bear the thought of giving up my marriage and family for the option of a life with another man.

Nevertheless, for the next three years I struggled in the dark, not knowing what to do or who to turn to for help. I thought it might help to talk things out with a therapist. I had a few visits with two different therapists, but both of them had already decided what was best for me and I didn't feel it would be an objective situation. The first couldn't understand the conflict I felt between these feelings and my religious and personal values. She suggested I simply accept myself as I was and do what felt good. She didn't encourage me to define what I wanted from life or work for anything better. The other therapist told me within the first few minutes of my first session that my religious values were my obvious problem and that they should be discarded. But I couldn't simply dismiss the values and beliefs that I held so deeply.

During these three years, I fell in and out of love with several men. One of them seemed to be "Mr. Right," and I was seriously considering moving in with him three weeks after I met him. I was emotionally needy, and so caught up in the positive strokes I got from him, that I thought I had found my perfect partner. I was willing to leave my wife, my children, and my church for a man I'd known for three weeks.

Finding My Way Out

Near my 34th birthday, I overheard a man talk about his work in counseling people with homosexual problems. When I called him a few weeks later, he told me that men were finding success in working with therapists and support groups. There were new theories in the psychological field that viewed homosexuality as an emotional issue and looked at the reasons behind the attractions. This made sense to me and I found hope. It eventually led me to answers to questions I had my whole life.

Therapy with this man was very helpful. Since I am a fairly analytical person, he helped me look at the situation objectively and weigh my options. I had someone to talk with and process ideas. I had someone I could trust to discuss these intimate issues. He was genuinely concerned about me and I didn't worry about being manipulated, like I did with the previous therapists I had visited.

We explored the relationships I had. It helped me see how fulfilling or unfulfilling they were and what I wanted from relationships. I realized this was a major deficit for me and I made plans to develop the kind of relationships I realized I needed. We talked about relationship skills and how to interact with other men. I realized that I unconsciously pushed people away, and my therapist gave me support and ideas on the skills I needed to build. After I practiced some skills and found success, my confidence grew and I reached out more.

Support Group

My therapist suggested I attend a self-help support group of other men who were also struggling with unwanted homosexual feelings. I attended the Phoenix group for a while, then Evergreen just after it was formed in 1989. The support group experience helped me open up on an emotional level and relate with other men to a degree that I had never done before. It was a protected, safe environment with other men who knew my deep, dark secrets and had the same deep, dark secrets. I could open up with them in a safe practice environment, then later apply it with straight men in the real world.

The men in my support group understood my feelings and helped me find solutions to my problems. When I felt depressed, I called them and they talked me out of desires to act sexually. I became good friends with several of them and knew they were genuinely concerned about me and I was genuinely concerned about them. I relied on them many times and never would have made it without their love and support. I had some great growing experiences in the three and a half years I attended support group meetings. . . .

What I Learned

Through this experience, I learned that my homosexuality was caused by many factors. There may have been some biological predisposition, but that doesn't seem to be a large factor for many people, and it appears that, for me, personality and environment played the major roles. I was a fairly sensitive boy. I needed a lot of peer support and relationships, and had very little of either growing up.

I also learned that my homosexuality was not essentially a sexual problem—it was an emotional one. My problems existed because basic, normal emotional needs were not being met. I learned that many men with homosexual problems have deficits relating with other men. Like me, they feel that somehow they never quite fit in as "one of the guys." So I tried (consciously or subconsciously) to fill unmet emotional needs in any way [I] could. I had normal, healthy needs to relate with other men, to feel accepted by them, and to be affirmed by them, but things got in the way as I grew up and the needs didn't get met. Even though I became an adult chronologically, I was still a teenager emotionally and had relationship needs that still needed to be filled.

Once I figured out what the issues were for me and began to take care of the underlying emotional deficits, the attractions and sexual compulsions decreased. When I found healthy, non-sexual ways to take care of the emotional needs, I didn't need to look

In a discussion of his own experiences, the author explains that his sexual attraction for men ceased once he addressed his underlying emotional needs. He then became able to enjoy platonic friendships with men.

at pictures of men or find some stranger to connect with. What I really wanted and needed were legitimate friendships with men. Once I fulfilled the underlying emotional needs, the homosexual desires disappeared.

Meeting Emotional Needs with Men and Women

I discovered that I have some needs that can be met only by other men. I need to bond with men and be affirmed by them. I need close buddies I can relate to and do things with on a male level. I also have needs that can be met only by women. Every man needs both men and women because of the complementary nature of the two genders. Men will never be totally fulfilled if they relate exclusively with other men; women bring a necessary component to the equation. There is something about the Mars-Venus concept that naturally attracts men and women together because it helps us grow, gives us balance, and makes us whole.

I also learned that this is a difficult process that takes time. Attitudes and experiences developed over decades can't usually be turned around in months. When I finally began to confront my problems and make up for the deficits, I was on an emotional roller coaster because I was opening up emotionally, confronting new issues, and experiencing some feelings for the first time. I went from highs to lows—sometimes within hours.

Time was condensed; I was growing emotionally perhaps a year every month or two. I was trying to build relationships with other men, initially with those in my support group who had the same kinds of emotional deficits I did. In many ways, I was growing emotionally in areas I should have experienced back in my teenage years, and it was difficult to do some things as an adult that should have been done when I was an adolescent.

The journey has been the hardest thing I've ever done, but it was worth it. Today, I am a different man—stronger, healthier, happier, more loving, more confident, more mature. I am a better father, a better husband, a better friend, and a more devoted son of God. I would never trade the peace, growth and healing I have experienced for anything in the world.

SIX

There Is No Evidence That Sexual Orientation Can Be Changed

Wayne Besen

Responding to a report released by the American Psychological Association that found "reparative therapy" designed to change sexual orientation does not work, Wayne Besen discusses in the following viewpoint the case of a gay man who attempted to become straight. According to Besen, the gay patient experienced mental suffering due to scare tactics and "treatments" he endured during his therapy sessions with an unethical "ex-gay" therapist. He stresses that "reparative therapy" is more harmful than helpful because it denies the gay client a nonjudgmental atmosphere. Besen is the founder and executive director of Truth Wins Out, an organization that fights antigay religious extremism.

There is "no evidence that sexual orientation change efforts work." This was the American Psychological Association's [APA's] verdict on "ex-gay" therapy after an appointed task force of experts studied the issue for two years.

The conclusion did not surprise those of us who work with people who have been harmed by such programs. For example, I just interviewed Patrick McAlvey, who entered therapy to change his sexual orientation at the age of 19. His counselor, Mike

Jones, is the director of Corduroy Stone, an affiliate of Exodus International.

Reparative Therapy

McAlvey says that his sessions included prolonged hugs, the suggestion that he use handyman tools to increase his masculinity and questions about the size of his genitalia. There was also an episode of "holding therapy" where he reclined into the lap of his supposedly "ex-gay" counselor for an hour. The goal, according to McAlvey, was to get comfortable with his own manliness by "feeling the strength" and "smelling the smell" of another man.

What Jones and other ex-gay counselors routinely call "therapy" can seem a great deal like foreplay to the rest of us.

"Ex Gay," cartoon by Peter Welleman. www.CartoonStock.com.

"I think it does a lot of damage to people's mental health," said McAlvey. "If I had had a fair representation (of gay life) I could have avoided a lot of suffering."

Of course, such therapy and ministry programs can only exist by grossly distorting the lives of gay people. For example, in a recent radio interview, ex-gay activist Charlene Cothran claimed that gay people do not want legal equality and are really only interested in the "freedom to be a homosexual in a park with no clothes on."

Alan Chambers, president of Exodus International, defends his organization's reparative therapy approach that claims to change the sexual orientation of gays. However, a 2009 report by the American Psychological Association concluded that reparative therapy is ineffective.

Taking Ex-gay Therapists to Task

The APA deserves credit for taking ex-gay therapists to task for twisting the truth and holding them accountable for their scare tactics, such as claiming that there are no happy gay people.

"The limited published literature on these programs suggests that many do not present accurate scientific information regarding same-sex sexual orientations to youth and families, are excessively fear-based and have the potential to increase sexual stigma," said the APA report, "Appropriate Therapeutic Responses to Sexual Orientation."

It was encouraging to see the APA question the ex-gay tactic of teaching vulnerable clients to live in a fantasy world. Groups like Exodus and the National Association for Research and Therapy of Homosexuality (NARTH), regularly encourage clients to say they have converted, even though they are still gay. The idea is that by proclaiming a false heterosexual identity in advance of any legitimate change, the desired transformation will eventually come.

This idea is equivalent to me wanting to play professional basketball, so I begin to identify as a member of the New York Knicks. Never mind that I am too short, too old and not good enough to make the roster. If I embrace this surreal existence long enough, I will one day be dunking the ball under the bright lights of Madison Square Garden.

SEVEN

Same-Sex Marriage Would Undermine the Institution of Marriage

Witherspoon Institute

The Witherspoon Institute is an independent research center in Princeton, New Jersey. In the following report, which was signed by more than seventy college professors, the authors maintain that marriage is a union between one man and one woman. The institution of marriage is good not only for the husband and wife, they say, but also for the common good of society, because it is the ideal way to raise children. Same-sex marriage is a threat to procreation and child-rearing and to the idea that children need both a mother and a father. Therefore, the authors contend, same-sex marriage is a threat to the institution of marriage.

In recent years, marriage has weakened, with serious negative consequences for society as a whole. Four developments are especially troubling: divorce, illegitimacy, cohabitation, and same-sex marriage. . . .

The Case for Marriage

Marriage protects children, men and women, and the common good. The health of marriage is particularly important in a free society, which depends upon citizens to govern their private lives and rear their children responsibly, so as to limit the scope, size, and power of the state. The nation's retreat from marriage has been particularly consequential for our society's most vulnerable communities: minorities and the poor pay a disproportionately heavy price when marriage declines in their communities. Marriage also offers men and women as spouses a good they can have in no other way: a mutual and complete giving of the self. Thus, marriage *understood as the enduring union of husband and wife is both a good in itself and also advances the public interest.*

We affirm the following ten principles that summarize the value of marriage—a choice that most people want to make, and that society should endorse and support.

Ten Principles on Marriage and the Public Good

1. Marriage is a personal union, intended for the whole of life, of husband and wife.
2. Marriage is a profound human good, elevating and perfecting our social and sexual nature.
3. Ordinarily, both men and women who marry are better off as a result.
4. Marriage protects and promotes the well-being of children.
5. Marriage sustains civil society and promotes the common good.
6. Marriage is a wealth-creating institution, increasing human and social capital.
7. When marriage weakens, the equality gap widens, as children suffer from the disadvantages of growing up in homes without committed mothers and fathers.
8. A functioning marriage culture serves to protect political liberty and foster limited government.
9. The laws that govern marriage matter significantly.
10. "Civil marriage" and "religious marriage" cannot be rigidly or completely divorced from one another.

This understanding of marriage is not narrowly religious, but the cross-cultural fruit of broad human experience and reflection,

State Laws on Same-Sex Marriage

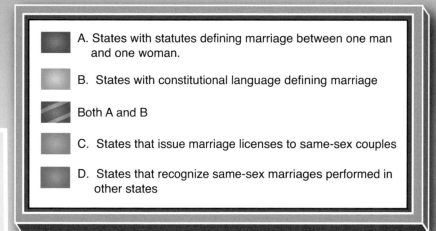

A. States with statutes defining marriage between one man and one woman.

B. States with constitutional language defining marriage

Both A and B

C. States that issue marriage licenses to same-sex couples

D. States that recognize same-sex marriages performed in other states

Legislative and Judicial Actions
Regarding Same-Sex Marriage

In 1998 Hawaii's constitution was amended to read, "The Legislature shall have the power to reserve marriage to opposite-sex couples." The Hawaii legislature subsequently passed a law prohibiting marriage for same-sex couples.

In October 2008 the Connecticut Supreme Court invalidated the state statute banning same-sex marriage.

In April 2009 the Iowa Supreme Court invalidated the state statute banning same-sex marriage.

In 2009 the District of Columbia passed a statute allowing same-sex marriage.

In 2009 New Hampshire passed legislation to allow same-sex marriages.

In August 2010 a federal district court invalidated California's constitutional provision banning same-sex marriage. The ban remains in place pending appeal.

In June 2011 New York passed a statute allowing same-sex marriage.

Taken from: National Conference of State Legislatures, "Same-Sex Marriage, Civil Unions and Domestic Partnorships, 2010. www.ncsl.org/default.aspx?tabid=16430.

and supported by considerable social science evidence. But a marriage culture cannot flourish in a society whose primary institutions—universities, courts, legislatures, religions—not only fail to defend marriage but actually undermine it both conceptually and in practice. . . .

The Challenge to Marriage

Marriage—considered as a legally sanctioned union of one man and one woman—plays a vital role in preserving the common good and promoting the welfare of children. In virtually every known human society, the institution of marriage provides order and meaning to adult sexual relationships and, more fundamentally, furnishes the ideal context for the bearing and rearing of the young. The health of marriage is particularly important in a free society such as our own, which depends upon citizens to govern their private lives and rear their children responsibly, so as to limit the scope, size, and power of the state. Marriage is also an important source of social, human, and financial capital for children, especially for children growing up in poor, disadvantaged communities who do not have ready access to other sources of such capital. Thus, from the point of view of spouses, children, society, and the polity, marriage advances the public interest.

But in the last forty years, marriage and family have come under increasing pressure from the modern state, the modern economy, and modern culture. Family law in all fifty states and most countries in the Western world has facilitated unilateral divorce, so that marriages can be easily and effectively terminated at the will of either party. Changing sexual mores have made illegitimacy and cohabitation a central feature of our social landscape. The products of Madison Avenue and Hollywood often appear indifferent to, if not hostile toward, the norms that sustain decent family life. New medical technology has made it easier for single mothers and same-sex couples to have children not only outside of marriage, but even without sexual intercourse. Taken together, marriage is losing its preeminent status as the social institution that directs and organizes reproduction, childrearing, and adult life. . . .

Same-Sex Marriage Weakens Traditional Marriage

Although the social scientific research on same-sex marriage is in its infancy, there are a number of reasons to be concerned about the consequences of redefining marriage to include same-sex relationships. First, no one can definitively say at this point how children are affected by being reared by same-sex couples. The current research on children reared by them is inconclusive and underdeveloped—we do not yet have any large, long-term, longitudinal studies that can tell us much about how children are affected by being raised in a same-sex household. Yet the larger empirical literature on child well-being suggests that the two sexes bring different talents to the parenting enterprise, and that children benefit from growing up with both biological parents.

Opponents of same-sex marriage say that marriage is a union between a man and a woman. They believe that same-sex marriage is a threat to procreation and to good child-rearing.

This strongly suggests that children reared by same-sex parents will experience greater difficulties with their identity, sexuality, attachments to kin, and marital prospects as adults, among other things. But until more research is available, the jury is still out.

Yet there remain even deeper concerns about the institutional consequences of same-sex marriage for marriage itself. Same-sex marriage would further undercut the idea that procreation is intrinsically connected to marriage. It would undermine the idea that children need both a mother and a father, further weakening the societal norm that men should take responsibility for the children they beget. Finally, same-sex marriage would likely corrode marital norms of sexual fidelity, since gay marriage advocates and gay couples tend to downplay the importance of sexual fidelity in their definition of marriage. Surveys of men entering same-sex civil unions in Vermont indicate that 50 percent of them do not value sexual fidelity, and rates of sexual promiscuity are high among gay men. For instance, Judith Stacey, professor of sociology at New York University and a leading advocate of gay marriage, hopes that same-sex marriage will promote a "pluralist expansion of the meaning, practice, and politics of family life in the United States" where "perhaps some might dare to question the dyadic limitations of Western marriage and seek some of the benefits of extended family life through small group marriages. . . ."

Our concerns are only reinforced by the legalization of same-sex marriage in Belgium, Canada, the Netherlands, and Spain—and its legalization in the Commonwealth of Massachusetts. Same-sex marriage has taken hold in societies or regions with low rates of marriage and/or fertility. For instance, Belgium, Canada, Massachusetts, the Netherlands, and Spain all have fertility rates well below the replacement level of 2.1 children per woman. These are societies in which child-centered marriage has ceased to be the organizing principle of adult life. Seen in this light, same-sex marriage is both a consequence of and further stimulus to the abolition of marriage as the preferred vehicle for ordering sex, procreation, and child-rearing in the West. While there are surely many unknowns, what we do know suggests that embracing same-sex marriage would further weaken marriage itself at the very moment when it needs to be most strengthened.

EIGHT

Same-Sex Marriage Does Not Harm Heterosexual Marriage

Theodore B. Olson

In June 2008 the California Supreme Court ruled that same-sex marriage was legal in California. In November of that year, California voters passed a constitutional amendment known as Proposition 8 that limited marriage to one man and one woman. Same-sex marriages performed in the state during the five months that such marriage had been legal remain valid. Several gay couples sued the state, challenging the constitutionality of the amendment. The case known as *Perry v. Schwarzenegger* was tried in early 2010. The judge ruled that Prop 8 was unconstitutional, but no same-sex marriages could be performed pending an appeal. The following viewpoint is from the closing argument in *Perry*. In his argument, Theodore B. Olson, the lead attorney for gay couples seeking to overturn Proposition 8, argues that marriage is a fundamental right. To deny same-sex couples the right to marry is discriminatory, much like the laws that prohibited mixed-race couples from marrying prior to the 1960s, he contends. Olson notes that evidence presented during the trial shows that committed couples, their children, and society are all better off when the state encourages marriage for all couples. He stresses that permitting same-sex couples to marry would not discourage

Theodore B. Olson, "Closing Argument in *Perry v. Schwarzenegger*," US District Court, June 16, 2010, American Foundation for Equal Rights. www.afer.org.

heterosexual couples from marrying nor from having children. According to Olson, same-sex couples only want the same right granted to heterosexual couples—to marry the person they love.

We conclude this trial, Your Honor, where we began. This case is about marriage and equality.

Stigmatized as Unworthy

The fundamental constitutional right to marry has been taken away from the plaintiffs and tens of thousands of similarly situated Californians. Their state has rewritten its constitution in order to place them into a special disfavored category where their most intimate personal relationships are not valid, not recognized, and second rate. Their state has stigmatized them as unworthy of marriage, different and less respected.

Because marriage is at the heart and soul of this case, I want to immediately turn to the subject of marriage and what we have learned during this trial about what it means to be able to marry and then to have the right extinguished. . . .

The Institution of Marriage

The proponents of Proposition 8 see marriage as an institution of, by and for the state, and to promote procreation and the raising of children by their biological parents. An institution to promote the state's interest. . . .

At times during the trial, the proponents predicted grave consequences if same-sex marriage were to be legalized in California.

For example, you asked, "How does permitting same-sex couples to marry in any way diminish the procreative aspect or function of marriage, or denigrate the institution of marriage for heterosexuals?"

Lead counsel responded: "Your Honor, because it will change the institution. If the institution is deinstitutionalized," he said, "Mr. [David] Blankenhorn will testify that will likely lead to very real social harms, such as lower marriage rates and high rates of divorce and nonmarital cohabitation, with more children raised outside the marriage and separated from at least one of their parents." . . .

And proponents' counsel said—it came down to this—"Same-sex marriage is simply too novel an experiment to allow for any firm conclusions about its long-term effect on societal interests. They just don't know."

That is the essence of the case as it comes to the end of the trial and to the closing arguments. They just don't know whether same-sex marriage will harm the institution of heterosexual marriage.

And I submit that the overwhelming evidence in this case proves that we do know. And the fact is that allowing persons to marry someone of the same sex will not, in the slightest, deter heterosexuals from marrying, from staying married, or from having babies.

In fact, the evidence was from the experts that eliminating invidious restrictions on marriage strengthens the institution of marriage for both heterosexual and homosexual persons and their children. . . .

Taking Away a Right

Yes, heterosexual people are able independently to procreate. Homosexual people may have that same capacity, but in their relationships that is not something that occurs.

But we're talking about, because of that, taking away the right of an intimate relationship that the Supreme Court has called the right of privacy, the right of liberty.

And you'd have to explain or make some statement that allowing these other individuals that we represent here today to engage in the institution of marriage will somehow stop that procreation or stop people from getting married or cause them to get divorced.

That's one of the positions they took. And then they said they don't know. . . .

The US Supreme Court's View on Marriage

I think it's really important to set forth the prism through which this case must be viewed by the judiciary. And that is the perspective on marriage, the same subject that we're talking about, by the United States Supreme Court. . . .

The Supreme Court has said that: Marriage is the most important relation in life. Now that's being withheld from the plaintiffs. It is the foundation of society. It is essential to the orderly pursuit of happiness. It's a right of privacy older than the Bill of Rights and older than our political parties. One of the liberties protected by the Due Process Clause. A right of intimacy to the degree of being sacred. And a liberty right equally available to a person in a homosexual relationship as to heterosexual persons. That's the *Lawrence vs. Texas* case.

Marriage, the Supreme Court has said again and again, is a component of liberty, privacy, association, spirituality and autonomy. It is a right possessed by persons of different races, by persons in prison, and by individuals who are delinquent in paying child support.

It is the right of individuals, not an indulgence dispensed by the State of California, or any state, to favored classes of citizens which could easily be withdrawn if the state were to change its mind about procreation. In other words, it is a right belonging to Californians, to persons. It is not a right belonging to the State of California.

And the right to marry, to choose to marry, has never been conditioned on or tied to procreation. It hardly could be rooted in the state's interest in procreation, since the right to marry, in Supreme Court cases, has been invoked sustaining the right to contraceptives, to divorce, and just a few years ago in that *Lawrence* case to homosexuals. . . .

Dictating Whom Residents Can and Cannot Marry

Individuals, such as the plaintiffs in this case and those who are similarly situated, may not marry the person of their choice. We have a Three Strikes law in California. You can go to prison for life. But if you are homosexual, you can't get married. There's that category. The people that can get married. The people that can't get married.

There's 18,000 people that were married during that period that you described, and who are legally married. But if they get divorced or if they are widowed, they can't remarry. And they can't even remarry the same person, in the case of a divorce, because the Constitution wouldn't recognize it. . . .

The Most Important Relationship in Life

I think it's really important, given what the Supreme Court has said about marriage and what the proponents said about marriage, to hear what the plaintiffs have said about marriage and what it means to them, in their own words.

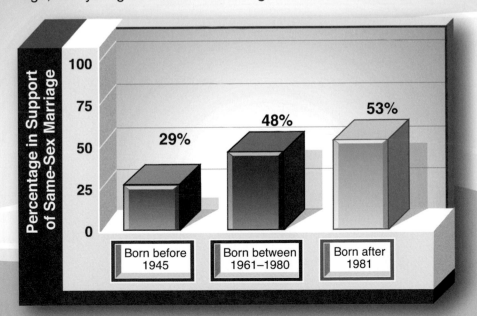

Support for Same-Sex Marriage Depends on Age

Support for same-sex marriage in 2010 was heavily dependent on age, with younger Americans favoring it more than older Americans.

Taken from: June Carbone and Naomi Cahn, "Class Actions," *Huffington Post*, February 4, 2011. www.huffingtonpost.com/june-carbone/class-actions-why-childre_b_818615.html.

They have said that marriage means—[that] this means not a domestic partnership. This means marriage, the social institution of marriage that is so valuable that the Supreme Court says it's the most important relation in life.

The plaintiffs have said that marriage means to them freedom, pride. These are their words. Dignity. Belonging. Respect. Equality. Permanence. Acceptance. Security. Honor. Dedication. And a public commitment to the world.

One of the plaintiffs said, "It's the most important decision you make as an adult." Who could disagree with that? . . .

Racial Restrictions Eliminated

We learned, also during the trial, that racial restrictions on the right to marry were finally eliminated for good in *Loving vs. Virginia* in 1967, ending laws like Proposition 8 which prohibited certain marriage choices for citizens that had once existed in 41 states.

Proposition 8 is very, very much like those restrictions, [expert witness] Dr. [Nancy] Cott explained, because it prevents a complete choice as to marriage and designates gays and lesbians as less worthy and entitled to less honor, less status and fewer benefits.

Marriage is special, the experts tell us. Domestic partnerships and civil unions are pale comparisons. As Dr. Cott put it, there is nothing that is like marriage except marriage. And the state's approval lends prestige and acceptance to the institution. . . .

Strengthening Marriage

The experts testified not only that same-sex marriage would not harm the institution of marriage or diminish heterosexual interest in marriage, they explained, as well, that the elimination of discriminatory barriers to marriage and harmful stigmas would, as it has in the past, strengthen the institution of marriage and strengthen our country.

We are not talking, just talking, about the couples who wish to get married. We are talking about their children.

In 2005, there were 37,000 of California's children living in households headed by same-sex couples. The evidence was uncontradicted during this trial and overwhelming that the lives of these children would be better if they were living in a marital household.

Even Mr. Blankenhorn, the proponents' witness, proponents' principal witness, agreed with that proposition. . . .

That is the [proponents'] principal expert witness, [who said] that approving same-sex marriage would be likely to improve the well-being of gay and lesbian households and their children.

I was stricken by Mr. Blankenhorn's testimony about the other societal benefits that would arise from permitting gays and lesbians to marry.

The Social Benefits

Mr. Blankenhorn admitted on the witness stand that same-sex marriage would yield numerous social benefits. . . .

He testified that it would decrease the number of those in society who would be viewed wearily as "other." In other words, not okay. And the elimination of that stigma and that discrimination, according to Mr. Blankenhorn, would be a victory for the American idea. . . .

The proponents' principal witness believes that gay and lesbian individuals would be better off, their children would be better off, we would be closer to the American ideal or the American idea in applying, he said, the principle of equal human dignity upon which this country was founded. "We will be more American the day we permit same-sex marriages." That is the proponents' principal witness. . . .

A Cherished Institution

So, Your Honor, it's important to emphasize, the plaintiffs have no interest in changing marriage or deinstitutionalizing marriage.

They desire to marry because they cherish the institution. They merely wish for themselves the status the State of California accords to their neighbors, to their friends, their coworkers, and their relatives.

The plaintiffs are in the same position as Mildred Jeter and Richard Loving, who in 1967 had no interest in diluting the institution of marriage. They only wanted to marry the person they loved, the person of their choice, who happened to be a person of a different race.

That's all the plaintiffs desire, the right to marry the person they love, the person of their choice, who happens to be of the same sex. . . .

Proponents of same-sex marriage contend that it is discriminatory to deny same-sex couples the fundamental right to marry someone they love.

Not a Reason

The latest words from . . . Counsel for the proponents is, "We don't know. We don't know whether there is going to be any harm."

And I would submit that, "We've always done it that way," that "It's a traditional definition of marriage". . . is the corollary to "Because I say so."

It's not a reason. You can't have continued discrimination in public schools because you have always done it that way. You can't have continued discrimination between races on the basis of marriage because you have always done it that way. That line of reasoning would have prevented the [Loving's] marriage. It would have justified racially segregated schools and maintaining subordinate status for married women. We heard a great deal about that relationship from Dr. Cott.

So the constitutional right to marry is fundamental. The constitutional right to be able to be in a relationship with a person of the same sex is a fundamental constitutional right. And in a sense, the State of California is burdening both of those—burdening in a very severe way that hurts individuals and it doesn't do any good to prevent those persons from getting married, because the evidence was also overwhelming in this regard.

Heterosexual people are not going to stop getting married. They are not going to abandon their marriage and they are not going to stop having children because their next door neighbor has a marriage [to] a person of the same sex. That is not going to happen. The evidence said that wasn't going to happen. . . .

A Discriminatory Law

I think, your Honor, that this law is discriminatory. The evidence is overwhelming that it imposes great social harm on individuals who are our equals. They are members of our society. They pay their taxes. They want to form a household. They want to raise their children in happiness and in the same way that their neighbors do.

We are imposing great damage on them by the institution of the State of California saying they are different and they cannot have the happiness, they cannot have the privacy, they cannot have the liberty, they cannot have the intimate association in the context of a marriage that the rest of our citizens do. We have demonstrated during this trial that that causes grave and permanent, irreparable and totally unnecessary harm, because we are withholding from them a part of the institution of marriage that we hold— . . . the language of one of those Supreme Court decisions is on the point—intimacy to the point of being sacred; that right of marriage in the context of the intimate relationship. We are [withholding] that from them, hurting them and we are doing no good. If we had a reason, a really good reason for inflicting all of that harm, that might be another matter, but there is no reason that I heard.

Preserving the institution of marriage. We've improved the institution of marriage when we allowed interracial couples to get married. We have improved the institution of marriage when we allowed women to be equal partners in the marital relationship. We have improved the institution of marriage when we didn't put artificial barriers based upon race. And we will improve the institution of marriage and we will be more American, according to Mr. Blankenhorn, when we eliminate this terrible stigma.

NINE

Civil Unions Are a Reasonable Alternative to Same-Sex Marriage

David Blankenhorn and Jonathan Rauch

In the following viewpoint David Blankenhorn and Jonathan Rauch argue that a compromise is needed for the issue of same-sex marriage. Instead of allowing same-sex marriage, they suggest that Congress should authorize same-sex civil unions with the provision that religious organizations would not have to perform these civil unions nor recognize them as marriages if these actions go against their beliefs. Most Americans would be more accepting of civil unions rather than same-sex marriage, and with such unions, gays would receive all the rights and benefits of marriage, lacking only the label of *marriage*. Blankenhorn is president of the Institute for American Values and the author of *The Future of Marriage*. Rauch is a guest scholar at the Brookings Institution and the author of *Gay Marriage: Why It Is Good for Gays, Good for Straights, and Good for America*.

In politics, as in marriage, moments come along when sensitive compromise can avert a major conflict down the road. The two of us believe that the issue of same-sex marriage has reached such a point now.

A Compromise

We take very different positions on gay marriage. We have had heated debates on the subject. Nonetheless, we agree that the time is ripe for a deal that could give each side what it most needs in the short run, while moving the debate onto a healthier, calmer track in the years ahead.

It would work like this: Congress would bestow the status of federal civil unions on same-sex marriages and civil unions granted at the state level, thereby conferring upon them most or all of the federal benefits and rights of marriage. But there would be a condition: Washington would recognize only those unions licensed in states with robust religious-conscience exceptions, which provide that religious organizations need not recognize same-sex unions against their will. The federal government would also enact religious-conscience protections of its own. All of these changes would be enacted in the same bill.

For those not immersed in the issue, our proposal may seem puzzling. For those deeply immersed, it may seem suspect. So allow us a few words by way of explanation.

Whatever our disagreements on the merits of gay marriage, we agree on two facts. First, most gay and lesbian Americans feel they need and deserve the perquisites and protections that accompany legal marriage. Second, many Americans of faith and many religious organizations have strong objections to same-sex unions. Neither of those realities is likely to change any time soon.

Protection for Religious Organizations

Further sharpening the conflict is the potential interaction of same-sex marriage with antidiscrimination laws. The First Amendment may make it unlikely that a church, say, would ever be coerced by law into performing same-sex wedding rites in its sanctuary. But religious organizations are also involved in many activities outside the sanctuary. What if a church auxiliary or charity is told it must grant spousal benefits to a secretary who marries her same-sex partner or else face legal penalties for discrimination based on sexual orientation or marital status? What

The mayor of Stamford, Connecticut, performs a civil union ceremony for a gay couple. The authors believe that civil unions are a good compromise between same-sex and traditional marriage.

if a faith-based nonprofit is told it will lose its tax-exempt status if it refuses to allow a same-sex wedding on its property?

Cases of this sort are already arising in the courts, and religious organizations that oppose same-sex marriage are alarmed. Which brings us to what we think is another important fact: Our national conversation on this issue will be significantly less contentious if religious groups can be confident that they will not be forced to support or facilitate gay marriage.

Concerns of Gay Couples

Gay couples have concerns of their own. Most, of course, want the right to marry, and nothing less. But federal recognition of same-sex marriage—leave aside what you think about the merits—is not likely in the near future. The federal Defense of Marriage Act forbids it. Barack Obama and most other Democratic presidential candidates opposed gay marriage. And most Americans continue to oppose it.

At the same time, federal law links many important perquisites to marital status, including Social Security survivor benefits, tax-free inheritance, spousal immigration rights and protections against mutual incrimination. All of these benefits are currently denied to same-sex couples, even those living in states that permit same-sex marriage or civil unions. But these same benefits could be conferred by federally recognized civil unions.

Yes, most gays are opposed to the idea that religious organizations could openly treat same-sex couples and opposite-sex couples differently, without fear of being penalized by the government. But we believe that gays can live with such exemptions without much difficulty. Why? Because most state laws that protect gays from discrimination already include some religious exemptions, and those provisions are for the most part uncontroversial, even among gays.

Civil Unions

And while most Americans who favor keeping marriage as it has customarily been would prefer no legal recognition of same-sex unions at either the federal or the state level, we believe that they can live with federal civil unions—provided that no religious groups are forced to accept them as marriages. Many of these people may come to see civil unions as a compassionate compromise. For example, a PBS poll last fall found that 58 percent of white evangelicals under age 30 favor some form of legal same-sex union.

Linking federal civil unions to guarantees of religious freedom seems a natural way to give the two sides something they would greatly value while heading off a long-term, take-no-prisoners conflict. That should appeal to cooler heads on both sides, and it also ought to appeal to President Obama, who opposes same-sex marriage but has endorsed federal civil unions. A successful template already exists: laws that protect religious conscience in matters pertaining to abortion. These statutes allow Catholic hospitals to refuse to provide abortions, for example. If religious exemptions can be made to work for as vexed a moral issue as abortion, same-sex marriage should be manageable, once reasonable people of good will put their heads together.

In all sharp moral disagreements, maximalism is the constant temptation. People dig in, positions harden and we tend to convince ourselves that our opponents are not only wrong-headed but also malicious and acting in bad faith. In such conflicts, it

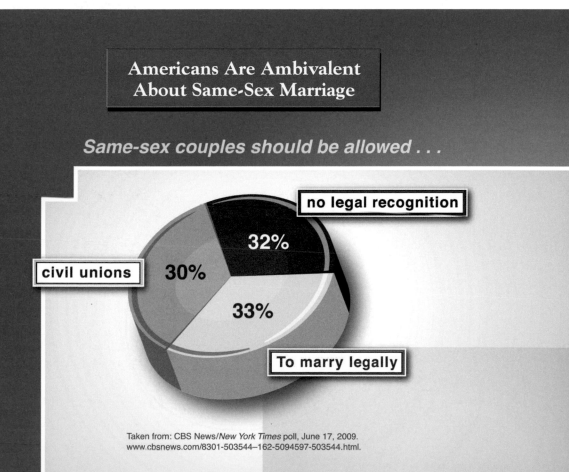

Americans Are Ambivalent About Same-Sex Marriage

Same-sex couples should be allowed . . .

no legal recognition — 32%

civil unions — 30%

To marry legally — 33%

Taken from: CBS News/*New York Times* poll, June 17, 2009.
www.cbsnews.com/8301-503544–162-5094597-503544.html.

can seem not only difficult, but also wrong, to compromise on a core belief.

But clinging to extremes can also be quite dangerous. In the case of gay marriage, a scorched-earth debate, pitting what some regard as nonnegotiable religious freedom against what others regard as a nonnegotiable human right, would do great harm to our civil society. When a reasonable accommodation on a tough issue seems possible, both sides should have the courage to explore it.

TEN

Civil Unions Make Homosexuals Second-Class Citizens

Douglas Sharp

> Douglas Sharp argues in the following viewpoint that civil
> unions, with all the rights, benefits, and privileges of mar-
> riage except for the name, create a second-class status. He
> points out that if a couple in a civil union relocates to a
> state where civil unions are not recognized, their rights,
> benefits, and privileges will end. Additionally a couple in
> a civil union do not qualify for federal benefits granted to
> married spouses, benefits that are recognized by all fifty
> states for married couples. Married couples have these
> rights because the government recognizes the importance
> of marriage. By denying these rights to couples in civil
> unions, Sharp asserts, the government is denying them
> equal rights. Sharp is dean of the Academy for the Common
> Good, a faith-based education series of Protestants for the
> Common Good, an advocacy organization.

Polling data both nationally and in Illinois make it evident
that a clear majority support civil unions though less than
half fully support same-sex marriage. At this moment, however,
I am wondering if this is a bill we should support.

Benefits of Civil Unions

This bill would make it possible for one partner in the union to make medical decisions for the other in the event of the latter's incapacitation. It would establish the right of one to access the other's benefits such as workers' compensation and pension. In the event of the wrongful death of one partner, the other would have standing and thus access to civil action. Should both parties to the union agree that it should come to an end, both parties are subject to laws that govern dissolution and disposition of property. The bill would make it possible for both partners to benefit from joint state tax returns and have standing in the disposition of wills, trusts and estates. The testimonial privilege now enjoyed by spouses would also apply to partners in a civil union, as would protections under the law against domestic violence.

There is much about this law that makes it comparable to those rights and privileges that pertain to a legal marriage. In fact, the law would make it possible for any adult couple, whether they are same-sex or different-sex, to partner in such a union. Arguably, it is a "marriage" of sorts; it just isn't called that.

Second-Class Status

But what it's called isn't really the problem. It's what it does that's the problem. Permitting and recognizing a particular set of rights, privileges and responsibilities as applicable to two people who freely consent to enter into such a relationship, in this case, effectively creates and sanctions a second-class status.

In the United States, people who marry in one state have a legal status that is recognized and protected in all the states of the Union. Should a couple in a lawful civil union in Illinois relocate to another state, all the rights and privileges accorded to them here would end. Unless the new state of residence recognized civil unions, the Illinois union would no longer be legally valid.

None of the federal laws pertaining to rights, privileges and benefits apply to the parties in an Illinois civil union. Should one lose employment and health coverage, COBRA health benefits would not be available for the other. The provisions of the Family

Many gays are against civil unions because they are not recognized from state to state. Moreover, federal laws do not grant gays the same benefits as those afforded to heterosexual married couples.

Medical Leave Act would not apply to the union, nor would exemptions from federal income and estate taxes. It would not be possible for one partner to receive the survivor portion of the other's Social Security benefit. Low-income partners in an Illinois civil union are ineligible to receive the federal Earned Income Tax Credit. If one of the partners is a homeowner, and together they choose to sell their home, the principal owner will have to file a capital gains tax calculated on the basis of a single rather than a married homeowner.

There are 1,138 benefits, rights and protections codified in federal law for married couples. Wherever a married couple lives or moves, these laws privilege their status as a couple and protect their financial interests at present and in the future.

The problem with civil unions in Illinois, then, is that creating them is a continuation of the denial of those rights accorded to married couples in identical relationship circumstances.

Marriage Has a Special Status

No reasonable person can deny that with marriage comes a special, respected, privileged, and beneficial status. From a social and cultural perspective, marriage can be defined any number of ways, and these definitions can be codified into law in order to protect the institution of marriage.

We practice marriage in the U.S. in ways and with rights, privileges and responsibilities that are different than those in Russia or Indonesia, Cambodia or Myanmar, Brazil or Germany. Our state and national governments identify and secure certain rights to the partners in a marriage because our society recognizes that the institution of marriage is extremely important. Indeed, the state has an interest in the institution of marriage because this institution is foundational to our social and economic fabric. Absent an interest in marriage, why would the state enact laws to manage it and protect those who enter into it?

In effect, this means that the state has an interest in encouraging and promoting stable and committed relationships. No married person would thrill at the prospect of having government interfere in any way in their relationship with their spouse. But those who are married most likely enjoy the fact that certain social and financial benefits accrue to them by government action. State and federal laws relative to the rights and privileges of marriage are in place because our government recognizes that a committed relationship, entered into by two persons with the intent of sharing life together and supporting one another, is a fundamental block in building a socioeconomic order; the social and economic unit established in such a relationship is foundational to establishing families, neighborhoods, and communities in which the flourishing of all is possible.

Equal Rights

But governments at all levels also have an interest in securing equal rights in our society. The principle of equality in our nation's history has not always been operative in our laws, but since our founding it has served as a criterion by which discriminatory laws have been overturned and more equitable laws established. And while social, economic and political debate can rage on the issue of equality of outcomes, no reasonable dissent can be offered on equal opportunity and the equal protection of the laws.

As a fundamental social and cultural institution in our society, marriage both reflects and secures this principle of equality, and it does so by affirming the freedom of choice. In its 1967 decision in *Loving v. Virginia*, which struck down Virginia's anti-miscegenation laws [laws that banned interracial marriage], the U.S. Supreme Court contended: "Marriage is one of the 'basic civil rights of man,' fundamental to our very existence and survival. To deny this fundamental freedom on so unsupportable a basis as the racial classifications embodied in these statutes, classifications so directly subversive of the principle of equality at the heart of the Fourteenth Amendment, is surely to deprive all the State's citizens of liberty without due process of law. The Fourteenth Amendment requires that the freedom of choice to marry not be restricted by invidious racial discriminations. Under our Constitution, the freedom to marry, or not marry, a person of another race resides with the individual and cannot be infringed by the State."

Marriage Is a Fundamental Right

In light of this and other decisions of the courts which have secured marriage as a fundamental human and civil right, it is both impracticable and unreasonable to deny this right to any citizen or lawful resident of the United States on the grounds of his or her sexual orientation. Regardless of one's view of the nature and origins of homosexual orientation and behavior, there is no justification for a government or state having a legal interest in an individual's sexual orientation; whether it is a matter of

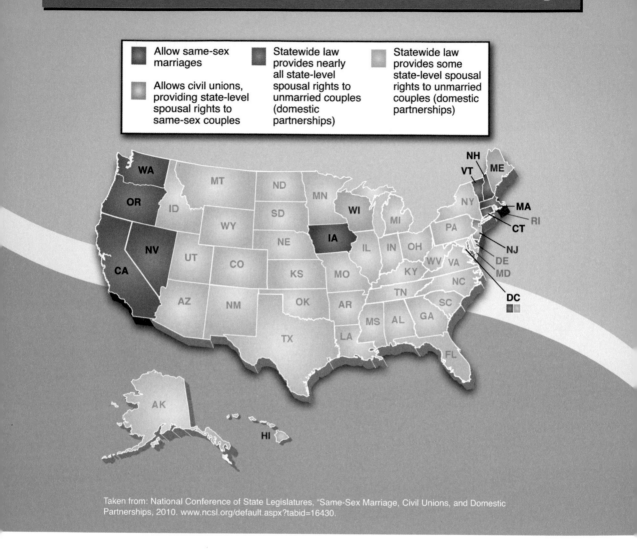

Allow same-sex marriages

Allows civil unions, providing state-level spousal rights to same-sex couples

Statewide law provides nearly all state-level spousal rights to unmarried couples (domestic partnerships)

Statewide law provides some state-level spousal rights to unmarried couples (domestic partnerships)

Taken from: National Conference of State Legislatures, "Same-Sex Marriage, Civil Unions, and Domestic Partnerships, 2010. www.ncsl.org/default.aspx?tabid=16430.

nature or nurture or both, it most assuredly is not a matter of state regulation or interference. If the state has no compelling interest in one's sexual orientation, the state has no basis to deny, on the basis of sexual orientation, civil rights guaranteed to others.

The U.S. Constitution and the Constitution of the state of Illinois have enshrined the principle of egalitarianism so that one cannot lawfully be denied his or her rights on the basis of one's race, religion, sex or place of origin.

Indeed, the principle of equality before the law entails an affirmation that all are equally subject to the law and all are equally beneficiaries of the law. But in this state, it is still possible to deny an individual the right to marry the person of his or her choice because the one chosen is of the same sex.

Not every couple in Illinois who freely chooses to love each other and commit to live together in all of life's circumstances, who wants to form a household and raise children and contribute out of their own personal and familial well-being to the improvement of their neighbors' lives and their community, who recognizes the social and economic importance of marriage and wishes to discharge their responsibilities and avail themselves of its benefits, not every such couple can get married in the state of Illinois. The adoption of civil unions will not change this. The one fact that prevents them from marrying is sexual orientation.

But it is not just the denial of one's right to marry the person of one's own choosing and benefit from the protections and privileges accorded to all married persons that renders a second-class status to civil unions. By any measure and by any definition—social, cultural, economic, emotional, spiritual—a civil union is not a marriage; it is, and by correlation always will be, a partnership that carries an inferior and disadvantaged status. In our society, it is marriage that stands as the definitive institutional expression of an intimate and committed interpersonal relationship, and civil unions do not carry the same social value and significance.

At best, civil unions are regarded by many as a pale imitation, a contrived and variable facsimile, of marriage. Granting same-sex couples the form of a sanctioned and protected relationship while different-sex couples enjoy the substance of a relationship whose reality is feigned in civil unions strikes me as both discriminatory and cruel.

Civil unions bring a measure of protection and benefit to same-sex couples in Illinois. But its enactment will not alter the fact that same-sex couples are treated differently under the law in Illinois, confined to a second-class status, and denied the equal protection of the law. For this reason, civil unions should be seen only as a stage on the way, a milestone to mark the advance toward the full inclusion and equality of all.

ELEVEN

The Repeal of "Don't Ask, Don't Tell" Will Have Little Impact on the US Military

Carter F. Ham and Jeh Charles Johnson

The risks to military readiness associated with overturning law and policies to allow gays to serve openly in the military are low, according to the authors of a report commissioned by the Department of Defense to study the "don't ask, don't tell" policy. The report notes that gay men and women already serve in the military, and most service members realize this. The authors of this viewpoint, Carter F. Ham and Jeh Charles Johnson, point out that over time the American military has successfully adapted to racial and gender integration, two changes that were strongly opposed at all levels of the military in the past. The authors conclude that if defense officials and military leaders allow the proper amount of time to train troops in preparation for the change, "don't ask, don't tell" can be successfully repealed. Ham, a general in the US Army, and Johnson, general counsel with the Department of Defense, led the forty-nine military service members and the nineteen civilians who made up the Comprehensive Working Group that studied the "don't ask, don't tell" policy.

Carter F. Ham and Jeh Charles Johnson, "Report of the Comprehensive Review of the Issues Associated with a Repeal of 'Don't Ask Don't Tell,'" US Department of Defense, November 30, 2010, pp. 1–2, 4–8, 17. www.defense.gov.

On March 2, 2010, the Secretary of Defense appointed the two of us to co-chair a working group to undertake a comprehensive review of the impacts of repeal, should it occur, of … the "don't ask, don't tell" law. . . .

A Survey of American Service Members

At the outset, it is important to note the environment in which we conducted our work: the Nation's military has been at war on several fronts for over 9 years. Much is being demanded from the force. The men and women in uniform who risk their lives to defend our Nation are, along with their families, stretched and stressed, and have faced years of multiple and lengthy deployments to Iraq, Afghanistan, and elsewhere. Some question the wisdom of taking on the emotional and difficult issue of "don't ask, don't tell" on top of all else. For these and other reasons, the Secretary directed that we "thoroughly, objectively and methodically examine all aspects of this question," and include, most importantly, the views of our men and women in uniform. Accordingly, over the last nine months we:

- solicited the views of nearly 400,000 active duty and reserve component Service members with an extensive and professionally-developed survey, which prompted 115,052 responses—one of the largest surveys in the history of the U.S. military;
- solicited the views of over 150,000 spouses of active duty and reserve component Service members, because of the influence and importance families play in the lives of Service members and their decisions to join, leave, or stay in the military, and received 44,266 responses;
- created an online inbox for Service members and their families to offer their views, through which we received a total of 72,384 entries;
- conducted 95 face-to-face "information exchange forums" at 51 bases and installations around the world, where we interacted with over 24,000 Service members—ranging from soldiers at Fort Hood, Fort Benning, and Fort Bragg, sailors at

Norfolk, San Diego, and Pearl Harbor, airmen at Lackland, Langley, and Yokota in Japan, Marines at Camp Lejeune, Camp Pendleton, and Parris Island, cadets and midshipmen at our Service academies, and Coast Guardsmen on Staten Island, New York;

- conducted 140 smaller focus group sessions with Service members and their families;
- solicited the views of the Service, academy superintendents and faculty, Service chiefs of chaplains, and Service surgeons general;
- solicited and received the views of various members of Congress;
- engaged RAND to update its 1993 study, *Sexual Orientation and U.S. Military Personnel Policy;*
- solicited and received the views of foreign allies, veterans groups, and groups both for and against repeal of the current law and policy; and
- during a two-week period prior to issuance, solicited and received the comments of the Secretaries of the Army, Navy and Air Force, and the Chiefs of each Service, on this report in draft form.

Finally, we heard the views and experiences of current and former Service members who are gay or lesbian. We knew that their viewpoints would be important, and we made affirmative efforts to reach them, though our ability to do so under the current "don't ask, don't tell" law was limited. The two of us personally interviewed former Service members who are gay or lesbian, including those who had been separated under "don't ask, don't tell." . . .

The Risk to Military Readiness Is Low

Based on all we saw and heard, our assessment is that . . . the risk of repeal of "don't ask, don't tell" to overall military effectiveness is low. We conclude that, while a repeal of "don't ask, don't tell" will likely, in the short term, bring about some limited and isolated disruption to unit cohesion and retention, we do not believe this disruption will be widespread or long-lasting. . . . Longer term, with a continued and sustained commitment to core values of leadership, professionalism, and respect for all, we are convinced that the U.S. military can adjust and accommodate this change, just as it has others in history. . . .

Survey Results

Consistently, the survey results revealed a large group of around 50–55% of Service members who thought that repeal of "don't ask, don't tell" would have mixed or no effect; another 15–20% who

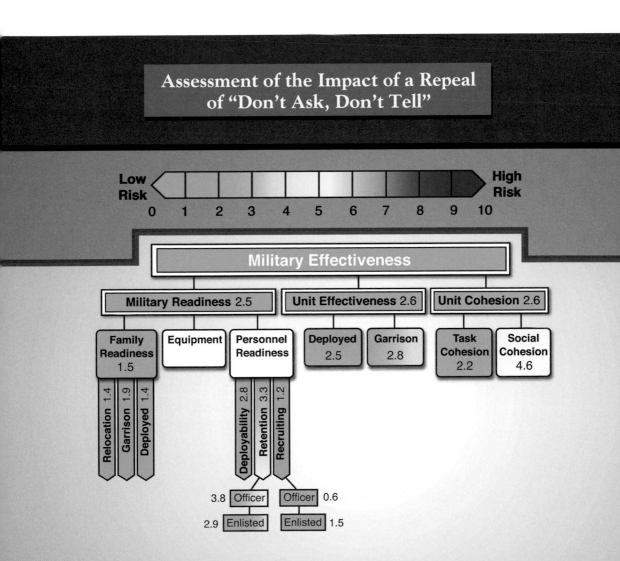

Taken from: Carter F. Ham and Jeh Charles Johnson, *Report of the Comprehensive Review of the Issues Associated with a Repeal of "Don't Ask, Don't Tell."* Washington, DC: Department of Defense, November 30, 2010.

said repeal would have a positive effect; and about 30% who said it would have a negative effect. The results of the spouse survey are consistent. When spouses were asked about whether repeal of "don't ask, don't tell" would affect their preference for their Service member's future plans to stay in the military, 74% said repeal would have no effect, while only 12% said "I would want my spouse to leave earlier."

To be sure, these survey results reveal a significant minority—around 30% overall (and 40–60% in the Marine Corps and in various combat arms specialties)—who predicted in some form and to some degree negative views or concerns about the impact of a repeal of "don't ask, don't tell." Any personnel policy change for which a group that size predicts negative consequences must be approached with caution. However, there are a number of other factors that still lead us to conclude that the risk of repeal to overall military effectiveness is low.

The reality is that there are gay men and lesbians already serving in today's U.S. military, and most Service members recognize this. As stated before, 69% of the force recognizes that they have at some point served in a unit with a co-worker they believed to be gay or lesbian. Of those who have actually had this experience in their career, 92% stated that the unit's "ability to work together" was "very good," "good," or "neither good nor poor," while only 8% stated it was "poor" or "very poor." Anecdotally, we also heard a number of Service members tell us about a leader, co-worker, or fellow Service member they greatly liked, trusted, or admired, who they later learned was gay; and how once that person's sexual orientation was revealed to them, it made little or no difference to the relationship. Both the survey results and our own engagement of the force convinced us that when Service members had the actual experience of serving with someone they believe to be gay, in general unit performance was not affected negatively by this added dimension.

"Open" Service

Yet, a frequent response among Service members at information exchange forums, when asked about the widespread recognition that gay men and lesbians are already in the military, were words to the effect of: "yes, but I don't *know* they are gay." Put another way, the concern with repeal among many is with "open" service.

In the course of our assessment, it became apparent to us that, aside from the moral and religious objections to homosexuality, much of the concern about "open" service is driven by misperceptions and stereotypes about what it would mean if gay Service members were allowed to be "open" about their sexual orientation. Repeatedly, we heard Service members express the view that "open" homosexuality would lead to widespread and overt displays of effeminacy among men, homosexual promiscuity, harassment and unwelcome advances within units, invasions of personal privacy, and an overall erosion of standards of conduct, unit cohesion, and morality. Based on our review, however, we conclude that these concerns about gay and lesbian Service members who are permitted to be "open" about their sexual orientation are exaggerated, and not consistent with the reported experiences of many Service members.

In today's civilian society, where there is no law that requires gay men and lesbians to conceal their sexual orientation in order to keep their job, most gay men and lesbians still tend to be discreet about their personal lives, and guarded about the people with whom they share information about their sexual orientation. We believe that, in the military environment, this would be true even more so. According to a survey conducted by RAND of a limited number of individuals who anonymously self-identified as gay and lesbian Service members, even if "don't ask, don't tell" were repealed, only 15% of gay and lesbian Service members would like to have their sexual orientation known to everyone in their unit. This conclusion is also consistent with what we heard from gay Service members in the course of this review. . . .

Predictions Versus Actual Experience

Given that we are in a time of war, the combat arms communities across all Services required special focus and analysis. Though the survey results demonstrate a solid majority of the overall U.S. military who predict mixed, positive or no effect in the event of repeal, these percentages are lower, and the percentage of those who predict negative effects are higher, in combat arms units. For example, . . . while the percentage of the overall U.S. military that predicts negative or very negative effects on their unit's ability to "work together to get the job done" is 30%, the percentage is 43% for the Marine Corps, 48% within Army combat arms units, and 58% within Marine combat arms units.

However, while a higher percentage of Service members in warfighting units *predict* negative effects of repeal, the percentage distinctions between warfighting units and the entire military are almost non-existent when asked about the *actual* experience of serving in a unit with someone believed to be gay. For example, when those in the overall military were asked about the experience of working with someone they believed to be gay or lesbian, 92% stated that their unit's "ability to work together," was "very good, "good" or "neither good nor poor." Meanwhile, in response to the same question, the percentage is 89% for those in Army combat arms units and 84% for those in Marine combat arms units—all very high percentages. Anecdotally, we heard much the same. As one special operations force warfighter told us, "We have a gay guy [in the unit]. He's big, he's mean, and he kills lots of bad guys. No one cared that he was gay."

Thus, the survey results reflecting actual experience, our other engagements, and the lessons of history lead us to conclude that the risks of repeal within warfighting units, while higher than the force generally, remain within acceptable levels when coupled with our recommendations for implementation. . . .

History Lessons

Our assessment here is also informed by the lessons of history in this country. Though there are fundamental differences between matters of race, gender, and sexual orientation, we believe the U.S. military's prior experiences with racial and gender integration are relevant. In the late 1940s and early 1950s, our military took on the racial integration of its ranks, *before* the country at large had done so. Our military then was many times larger than it is today, had just returned from World War II, and was in

In anticipation of the the repeal of the "don't ask, don't tell" policy, a US Marine officer conducts a training session to familiarize his men with the military's evolving position on gay and lesbian service members.

the midst of Cold War tensions and the Korean War. By our assessment, the resistance to change at that time was far more intense: surveys of the military revealed opposition to racial integration of the Services at levels as high as 80–90%. Some of our best-known and most-revered military leaders from the World War II era voiced opposition to the integration of blacks into the military, making strikingly similar predictions of the negative impact on unit cohesion. But by 1953, 95% of all African-American soldiers were serving in racially integrated units, while public buses in Montgomery, Alabama and other cities were still racially segregated: Today, the U.S. military is probably the most racially diverse and integrated institution in the country—one in which an African American rose through the ranks to become the senior-most military officer in the country 20 years before Barack Obama was elected President.

The story is similar when it came to the integration of women into the military. In 1948, women were limited to 2% of active duty personnel in each Service, with significant limitations on the roles they could perform. Currently, women make up 14% of the force, and are permitted to serve in 92% of the occupational specialties. Along the way to gender integration, many of our Nation's military leaders predicted dire consequences for unit cohesion and military effectiveness if women were allowed to serve in large numbers. As with racial integration, this experience has not always been smooth. But, the consensus is the same: the introduction and integration of women into the force has made our military stronger.

The general lesson we take from these transformational experiences in history is that in matters of personnel change within the military, predictions and surveys tend to overestimate negative consequences, and underestimate the U.S. military's ability to adapt and incorporate within its ranks the diversity that is reflective of American society at large.

Our Allies' Experiences

Our conclusions are also informed by the experiences of our foreign allies. To be sure, there is no perfect comparator to the U.S. military, and the cultures and attitudes toward homosexuality vary greatly among nations of the world. However, in recent times a number of other countries have transitioned to policies that permit open military service by gay men and lesbians. These include the United Kingdom, Canada, Australia, Germany, Italy, and Israel. Significantly, prior to change, surveys of the militaries in Canada and the U.K. indicated much higher levels of resistance than our own survey results—as high as 65% for some areas—but the actual implementation of change in those countries went much more smoothly than expected, with little or no disruption. . . .

In sum, we are convinced the U.S. military can make this change, even during this time of war.

TWELVE

"Don't Ask, Don't Tell" Should Not Be Repealed

John McCain

In the following viewpoint Arizona senator and former presidential candidate John McCain argues that the "don't ask, don't tell" policy, in which gays may serve in the military as long as they do not disclose their homosexuality, should not be overturned. He explains that military service members live and work in situations where there is little or no privacy, military rules and regulations include many restrictions on service members that would not be tolerated by civilians, and the key to military readiness is good order and unit cohesion. Allowing gays to serve openly, he asserts, would disrupt order and cohesion and would therefore threaten military readiness. McCain maintains that while "don't ask, don't tell" is an imperfect policy, it should not be overturned.

We meet to consider the "don't ask, don't tell" policy, a policy that the President [Barack Obama] has made clear, most recently last week in his [January 2010] State of the Union Address, that he wants Congress to repeal. This would be a substantial and controversial change to a policy that has been successful

John McCain, "Testimony, Department of Defense Authorization for Appropriations for Fiscal Year 2011, and to Receive Testimony Relating to the 'Don't Ask, Don't Tell' Policy," Tuesday, February 2, 2010, US Senate Committee on Armed Services, US Senate Committee on Armed Services, February 2, 2010, pp. 54–56. http://armed-services.senate.gov.

for 2 decades. It would also present yet another challenge to our military at a time of already tremendous stress and strain.

The Policy Should Not Be Repealed

Our men and women in uniform are fighting two wars, guarding the front lines against a global terrorist enemy, serving and sacrificing on battlefields far from home, and working to rebuild and reform the force after more than 8 years of conflict. At this moment of immense hardship for our armed services, we should not be seeking to overturn the "don't ask, don't tell" policy.

I want to make one thing perfectly clear up front. I'm enormously proud of and thankful for every American who chooses to put on the uniform of our Nation and serve at this time of war. I want to encourage more of our fellow citizens to serve and to open up opportunities to do so. Many gay and lesbian Americans are serving admirably in our armed forces, even giving their lives so that we and others can know the blessings of peace. I honor their sacrifice and I honor them.

Our challenge is how to continue welcoming this service amid the vast complexities of the largest, most expensive, most well-regarded, and most critical institution in our Nation, our armed forces. This is an extremely difficult issue and the Senate vigorously debated it in 1993. We heard from the senior uniformed and civilian leaders of our military on eight occasions before this committee alone. When Congress ultimately wrote the law, we included important findings that did justice to the seriousness of the subject. . . .

Three Important Points

I won't quote all those findings, but three points must be made. First, Congress found in the law that the military's mission to prepare for and conduct combat operations requires service men and women to accept living and working conditions that are often spartan and characterized by forced intimacy with little or no privacy.

Second, the law finds that civilian life is fundamentally different from military life, which is characterized by its own laws, rules,

US Combat Troops Oppose Gays in the Military

This graph shows the responses of US combat troops to the following question: *If "don't ask, don't tell" is repealed, and you are working with a service member in your immediate unit who has said he or she is gay or lesbian, how, if at all, would it affect your immediate unit's effectiveness in completing its mission in a field environment or out to sea?*

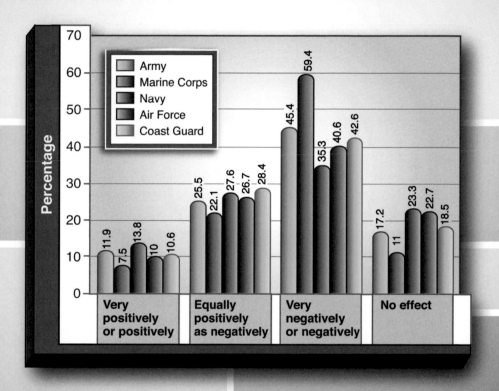

Taken from: Carter F. Ham and Jeh Charles Johnson, *Report of the Comprehenisve Review of the Issues Associated with a Repeal of "Don't Ask, Don't Tell."* Washington DC: Department of Defense, November 30, 2010.

customs, and traditions, including many restrictions on personal conduct that would not be tolerated in civil society.

Finally, the law finds that the essence of military capability is good order and unit cohesion and that any practice which puts those goals at unacceptable risk can be restricted.

These findings were the foundation of "don't ask, don't tell" and I'm eager to hear from our distinguished witnesses what has changed since these findings were written such that the law they supported can now be repealed.

Not an Ideal Policy, but Effective

Has this policy been ideal? No, it has not, but it has been effective. It has helped to balance the potentially disruptive tension between the desires of a minority and the broader interests of our all-volunteer force. It is well understood and predominantly supported by our fighting men and women. It reflects, as I understand them, the preferences of our uniformed services. It has sustained unit cohesion and unit morale while still allowing gay and lesbian

John McCain, the ranking Republican on the Senate Armed Services Committee, is seen during hearings on the "don't ask, don't tell" policy in February 2010. McCain opposes repeal.

MR. McCAIN

Americans to serve their country in uniform. And it has done all of this for nearly 2 decades.

Mr. Chairman, [I present to you] a letter signed by over 1,000 former general and flag officers who have weighed in on this issue. I think that we all in Congress should pay attention and benefit from the experience and knowledge of over a thousand former general officers and flag officers, where they say: "We firmly believe that this law which Congress passed to protect good order, discipline and morale in the unique environment of the armed forces deserves continued support." So I think we should also pay attention to those who have served, who can speak more frankly on many occasions than those who are presently serving.

"Don't Ask, Don't Tell" Is Working

I know that any decision Congress makes about the future of this law will inevitably leave a lot of people angry and unfulfilled. There are patriotic and well-meaning Americans on each side of this debate, and I have heard their many passionate concerns. Ultimately, though, numerous military leaders tell me that "don't ask, don't tell" is working and that we should not change it now. I agree.

I would welcome a report done by the Joint Chiefs of Staff based solely on military readiness, effectiveness, and needs, and not on politics, that would study the "don't ask, don't tell" policy, that would consider the impact of its repeal on our armed services, and that would offer their best military advice on the right course of action.

We have an all-volunteer force. It is better trained, more effective, and more professional than any military in our history, and today that force is shouldering a greater global burden than at any time in decades. We owe our lives to our fighting men and women and we should be exceedingly cautious, humble, and sympathetic when attempting to regulate their affairs.

"Don't ask, don't tell" has been an imperfect but effective policy, and at this moment, when we're asking more of our military than at any time in recent memory, we should not repeal this law.

What You Should Know About Homosexuality

Americans' Views on Homosexuality

According to a May 2010 Gallup Poll:

- For the first time, more than 50 percent of Americans believe gay and lesbian relations are morally acceptable.
- The percentage of Americans who believe homosexuality is morally wrong dropped to 43 percent in 2010, a steady decline since a high of 55 percent in 2002.
- Men in general, and specifically men between the ages of eighteen and forty-nine, are the most accepting of homosexuality, with 62 percent and 53 percent, respectively, finding it morally acceptable.
- Fifty-one percent of women of all ages find gay and lesbian relations morally acceptable, while 59 percent of women between the ages of eighteen and forty-nine believe so.

Factors Contributing to Homosexuality

According to the May 2010 Gallup Poll:

- Thirty-seven percent of Americans believe being gay is due to a person's upbringing and environment.
- Americans' views on the causes of homosexuality have changed gradually since the 1970s and 1980s, when more than 50 percent of Americans believed it was due to upbringing and environment.

- The percentage of Americans who believe that homosexuality is a trait a person is born with has remained fairly steady during the past decade, fluctuating between 34 percent and 39 percent.

Same-Sex Marriage

According to the National Conference of State Legislatures:

- In 1993 the Hawaii Supreme Court ruled that denying same-sex marriage couples the right to marry was unconstitutional unless the state can present a "compelling state interest" to justify the ban.
- As of 2011 five states—Connecticut, Iowa, Massachusetts, New Hampshire, and Vermont—and the District of Columbia allow same-sex couples to marry.
- In California same-sex couples were allowed to marry for a brief period—between June and November 2008—until voters there passed Proposition 8, the constitutional amendment that banned same-sex marriage. The unions of gay couples who married in that time period are recognized by the state of California.
- Proposition 8 was passed with 52 percent of the voters in favor of the amendment.
- Ten countries legally recognize same-sex marriage: Argentina, Belgium, Canada, Iceland, Netherlands, Norway, Portugal, South Africa, Spain, and Sweden.

Gays in the Military

According to the 2010 *Report of the Comprehensive Review of the Issues Associated with a Repeal of Don't Ask, Don't Tell:*

- Sixty percent of military service members polled said that working with a service member who is gay or lesbian would have no effect on their personal readiness.
- A majority (51.5 percent) of service members said a gay or lesbian service member would have no effect on their individual efforts to train well.
- Just over 46 percent of troops polled said that a gay or lesbian service member would have no effect on their unit's readiness,

while 21.2 percent said gay or lesbian service members would affect the unit's readiness.

- The percentage of service members who felt a gay or lesbian service member would have no effect on their unit's ability to train well was 37.1 percent, with 31.3 percent saying it would have a negative or very negative effect.
- Among troops who have combat experience, more than 44 percent said a gay or lesbian service member would have a negative or very negative effect on their unit's effectiveness at completing its mission when the unit was training in the field or at sea.
- However, the percentage of troops with combat experience who believed a gay or lesbian service member would have a negative or very negative effect on the unit's ability to complete its mission in an intense combat situation dropped to 30.6 percent.

What You Should Do About Homosexuality

Homosexuality is a very divisive issue among people of all ages, races, faiths, political beliefs, and nationalities. In some countries in Africa and the Middle East it is a crime to be a homosexual, and a few countries even impose the death penalty on people convicted of being gay. Yet in Australia and in most countries in North and South America, and in Europe, homosexuality is legal, and several nations even allow gays and lesbians to marry.

Perhaps one reason for the vast differences in a culture's acceptance of homosexuality is due to whether or not that society believes people are "born gay." People in countries that are more accepting of homosexuality tend to believe that a person's sexual identity is present at birth, while societies that are less accepting of homosexuality have more conservative religious beliefs or are more likely to believe that people choose to be gay.

Although more than 50 percent of Americans in a May 2010 Gallup poll believe that homosexuality is morally acceptable, it is still difficult for some gay people, especially teens and young adults, to come to terms with their sexuality. Scott Quasha, a professor of school psychology at Brooklyn College, says in a December 2010 article in *Ladies' Home Journal*, "Despite recent cultural shifts, kids still get the overwhelming message from society that homosexuality is not acceptable." It can also be difficult for friends and family members to accept that their vision for a young adult's future—particularly concerning marriage and children—may not match what is envisioned by that person if he or she is gay. No matter how much parents may love their child and be accepting of homosexuality in the abstract, they may not know how to respond to homosexuality when faced with the announcement that their child is gay. When Deon Davis's fifteen-year-old son, Rashad, told her he was gay, "I took a big swallow. I forced myself to say 'okay' and hug him, but then I went off and cried all night long." When Rashad later told her his schoolmates were harassing him because he was gay, Davis said, "I knew I would have to be his protector and guide."[1]

If Someone You Know Is Gay

No matter what your beliefs about what causes or contributes to a person's sexual orientation, or about the morality of homosexuality, it can be difficult to accept the news that a friend or family member is gay. Some people may absolutely refuse to believe the assertion of homosexuality. Parents have envisioned their child's future for years, which usually includes a wedding and eventually children. It may be difficult for them to give up on these dreams, or to think of their child's spouse as being of the same gender, or of their grandchildren having two mommies or two daddies. Family members and friends may try to talk the gay teen out of being gay, convinced that he or she is mistaken about his or her feelings, or that he or she is just going through a phase. Some people may go into denial and refuse to discuss the issue; some might discourage the newly "out" teen from joining gay support groups.

You might believe you are protecting a gay friend or family member from harassment or bullying if you pretend he or she is straight. Or perhaps your religion teaches that homosexual relations are a sin and you feel you should distance yourself from those who are gay. Families and friends who pretend a gay teen is straight or are otherwise intolerant of his or her homosexuality may actually end up harming the youth, according to psychiatrists and social workers. A study published in the January 2010 *Pediatrics* journal found that gay, lesbian, and bisexual young adults whose families rejected their orientation were more than eight times more likely to commit suicide, nearly six times more likely to suffer from depression, and 3.4 times more likely to abuse drugs and have unprotected sex, compared to youth whose families were more accepting of their sexuality. In a press release about the *Pediatrics* study, Sten Vermund, a pediatrician and the Amos

Christie Chair of Global Health at Vanderbilt University, said, "This study clearly shows the tremendous harm of family rejection, even if parents think they are well intentioned, following deeply held beliefs or even protecting their children." Vermund and other experts say that families and friends should find some way to support the gay teen, even if it is just hugging him and telling him you love him and that you'll be there for him.

Tolerance

Gay teens and young adults may be accepted by their family and friends but may still be subject to harassment, bullying, or intolerance by other individuals and by organizations. Even those who are straight but are perceived to be gay are often subject to bullying. Some religious denominations, even though morally opposed to homosexuality, have spoken out against bullying, stating that every person, regardless of sexual orientation, deserves to be treated with dignity. Even Exodus International, a Christian organization that is morally opposed to homosexuality and that tries to help gays change their orientation, has modified its stance against homosexuality. Instead of urging its supporters to confront and speak out against homosexuals, it now advocates tolerance.

If you witness antigay bullying or harassment, it is important to take a stand. Tell the bully that such words and actions are unacceptable. Maureen Costello, director of Teaching Tolerance, a program of the Southern Poverty Law Center that provides information and resources about equality and justice, says, "We have to tell our children that bullying of any kind is unacceptable, but we also have to model the behavior we expect of them."[2] If you do not feel comfortable confronting the antagonist yourself, tell a teacher, parent or other responsible adult.

Examine Your Own Views

How do you feel about homosexuality? Do you think it is a sin? Would being gay affect how well someone could be a parent? Do you think gay marriage harms the institution of marriage, and if so, how? Should gays be allowed to marry or should marriage be restricted to those of the opposite sex only? Should gays be allowed to serve in the military? What do you think makes someone homosexual? Do you think you are gay? Can gays change their sexual identity and become straight? Should information about homosexuality and discussions about gays be taught in schools and religious institutions? Do homosexuals want "special rights" or "equal rights"?

If You Have Been the Victim of Antigay Harassment

If you feel you have been harassed because of your sexual orientation (or your perceived sexual orientation), you have several options. First of all, you can try talking to the offending party and let him or her know of your concerns. Such harassment is against the law in some states. In many cases, simply informing people that their actions may be breaking the law may be enough to get them to stop. If asking someone to stop does not work, you should let your parents, teachers, coach, or religious leader know you are being harassed, and they can take steps to stop the bullying.

Take a Stand

The articles in this volume will help you become more aware of the issues involved with homosexuality. Get to know your school's policies on bullying and harassment. Teachers, administrators, counselors, coaches, school nurses, religious leaders, and parents want to know if students are the subject of bullying due to their sexual identity. As you become more informed, you can take a stand on homosexuality in your school, church or temple, or neighborhood. If you find that school or religious authorities are turning a blind eye to antigay harassment, or if your school's or church's policies do not seem fair or reasonable, you might choose to speak up. If you speak up in a respectful and reasoned way, religious leaders, administrators, teachers, and parents are more likely to consider your thoughts and opinions. The Mental Health America organization suggests that students work with their student councils and school administrators to institute programs on respect, school safety, and antigay prejudice. In addition, it suggests that students start a chapter of the Gay, Lesbian, and Straight Education Network (GLSEN) at their school. A national survey found that teens whose schools had this club in their school felt safer and more accepted.

Notes

1. Quoted in Kenneth Miller, "Gay Teens Bullied to the Point of Suicide," *Ladies' Home Journal*, December 2010. www.lhj.com/relationships/family/raising-kids/gay-teens-bullied-to-suicide.
2. Quoted in Miller, "Gay Teens Bullied to the Point of Suicide."

The editors have compiled the following list of organizations concerned with the issues debated in this book. The descriptions are derived from materials provided by the organizations. All have publications or information available for interested readers. The list was compiled on the date of publication of the present volume; the information provided here may change. Be aware that many organizations take several weeks or longer to respond to inquiries, so allow as much time as possible for the receipt of requested materials.

Advocates for Youth
1025 Vermont Ave. NW, Ste. 200
Washington, DC 20005
(202) 347-5700 • fax: (202) 347-2263
e-mail: info@advocatesforyouth.org
website: www.advocatesforyouth.org

Advocates for Youth is a national organization focusing solely on sexuality issues among young people. It provides information, education, and advocacy to youth-serving agencies and professionals, policy makers, and the media. It supports federal legislation that addresses discrimination based on sexual orientation and/or gender identity.

American Civil Liberties Union (ACLU)
125 Broad St., 18th Fl.
New York, NY 10004
(212) 549-2500
website: www.aclu.org

The ACLU is the nation's oldest and largest civil liberties organization. Its Lesbian and Gay Rights/AIDS Project, started in 1986, handles litigation, education, and public policy work on behalf of gays and lesbians. The ACLU publishes the handbook *The Rights of Lesbians and Gay Men*, as well as the monthly newsletter *Civil Liberties Alert*.

Concerned Women for America (CWA)
370 L'Enfant Promenade SW, Ste. 800
Washington, DC 20024
(202) 488-7000 • fax: (202) 488-0806
website: www.cwfa.org

The CWA's purpose is to preserve, protect, and promote traditional Judeo-Christian values through education, legislative action, and other activities. It seeks to create an environment that is conducive to building strong families and raising healthy children. It opposes homosexual relationships and gay marriage. The CWA publishes the monthly *Family Voice*, which periodically addresses such issues as homosexuality, same-sex marriage, and gays in the military.

Exodus International
PO Box 540119
Orlando, FL 32854
(407) 599-6872 or (888) 264-0877
website: www.exodusinternational.org

Exodus International is a nonprofit Christian organization that views homosexual identity, acts, and lifestyle as destructive and sinful behavior. The organization believes that homosexuals can be redeemed through Jesus Christ and that their homosexual attractions can be changed through self-determination and a personal relationship with God. It publishes the books *Homosexuality 101, God's Grace and the Homosexual Next Door,* and *You Don't Have to Be Gay.* Its website contains personal accounts of people who have changed their sexual orientation, as well as a blog.

Family Acceptance Project (FAP)
San Francisco State University
3004 Sixteenth St., Ste. 301
San Francisco, CA 94103

(415) 522-5558

e-mail: fap@sfsu.edu • website: http://familyproject.sfsu.edu

FAP, in collaboration with San Francisco State University, is a research, intervention, education, and policy initiative organization that works to decrease major health and related risks, such as suicide, substance abuse, HIV/AIDS, and homelessness, for lesbian, gay, bisexual, and transgender (LGBT) youth. FAP provides confidential support services to help families decrease rejection and increase support for their children who are LGBT, or who question their sexual identity. It publishes the pamphlet *Supportive Families, Healthy Children*, and sponsors research and articles about families and LGBT teens.

Family Research Council (FRC)

700 Thirteenth St. NW, Ste. 500

Washington, DC 20005

(202) 393-2100 • fax: (202) 393-2134

e-mail: corrdept@frc.org • website: www.frc.org

The FRC promotes the traditional family unit, which it defines as a union between a man and a woman. The council opposes gay marriage, gay adoption, and what it views as the public education system's tolerance of homosexuality. It publishes numerous reports from a conservative perspective, including the monthly newsletter *Washington Watch* and the bimonthly journal *Family Policy*.

Focus on the Family

8605 Explorer Dr.

Colorado Springs, CO 80995

(719) 531-3400 or (800) 232-6459 • fax: (719) 548-4525

website: www.family.org

Focus on the Family promotes Christian values and strong family ties. The organization campaigns against pornography, homosexual rights laws, prostitution, and sex trafficking. It publishes the monthly magazines *Focus on the Family* and *Focus on the Family*

Citizen. Its website offers opinion columns, news articles, reports, and links that address homosexuality.

Freedom to Marry
116 W. Twenty-Third St., Ste. 500
New York, NY 10011
(212) 851-8418 • fax: (646) 375-2069
website: www.freedomtomarry.org

Freedom to Marry is an organization that is working to educate the public about why marriage matters to same-sex couples, to increase the support for same-sex marriage, to earn the right for same-sex marriage in all fifty states, and to eliminate federal discrimination against same-sex marriage. It is partnering with individuals and organizations across the country to end the exclusion of same-sex couples from marriage and from the protections, responsibilities, and commitment that marriage brings. Its website contains a blog with articles about the organization's efforts to secure same-sex marriage, its strategy for increasing support for same-sex marriage, and a state-by-state status update of same-sex marriage.

Gay & Lesbian Alliance Against Defamation (GLAAD)
5455 Wilshire Blvd., Ste. 1500
Los Angeles, CA 90036
(323) 933-2240 • fax: (323) 933-2241
e-mail: info@glaad.org • website: www.glaad.org

GLAAD is a nonprofit organization dedicated to promoting understanding of and equality for the lesbian, gay, bisexual, and transgender (LGBT) community. GLAAD focuses in part on media representations' promoting fair and accurate coverage of the LGBT community. The website offers resources including the *Network Responsibility Index* and the *Media Reference Guide*.

The Heritage Foundation
214 Massachusetts Ave. NE
Washington, DC 20002-4999

(202) 546-4400 • fax: (202) 546-8328
e-mail: info@heritage.org • website: www.heritage.org

The Heritage Foundation is a public policy research institute that supports the ideas of limited government and the free-market system. Among other views, the foundation promotes the definition of marriage as between a man and a woman and opposes gays serving openly in the military. The website includes lectures, testimonies, and other essays on topics related to homosexuality.

It Gets Better Project
8315 Beverly Blvd., Ste. 101
Los Angeles, CA 90048
website: www.itgetsbetter.org

The It Gets Better Project was established in 2010 by gay columnist Dan Savage, who created a YouTube video to inspire hope for young people who are being harassed and bullied because of their sexual identity. His video inspired tens of thousands of other videos from celebrities, organizations, activists, politicians, and media personalities; these videos have been viewed more than 35 million times. The website aims to show gay, lesbian, bisexual, and transgendered teens and adults that love and happiness can be a reality in their future. The project allows people to add their stories to the website.

Marriage Equality USA (MEUSA)
4096 Piedmont Ave., Ste. 257
Oakland, CA 94611
(510) 496-2700 • fax: (510) 380-5200
e-mail: info@marriageequality.org
website: www.marriageequality.org

MEUSA is a national grassroots organization with a mission to secure legally recognized civil marriage equality for all, at the federal and state level, without regard to gender identity or sexual orientation. It believes the most powerful way to persuade people to support marriage equality is to put real faces to the harms of marriage discrimination. MEUSA sponsors letter-writing campaigns, media events, press conferences, statewide rallies, and other high-profile events. Its website offers numerous fact sheets about marriage rights and links to books, movies, and other resources about same-sex marriage.

National Association for Research and Therapy of Homosexuality (NARTH)
(888) 364-4744
e-mail: info@narth.org • website: www.narth.org

NARTH is a nonprofit educational organization dedicated to affirming a male-female model of marriage and sexuality. The group includes psychiatrists, psychologists, certified social workers, professional and pastoral counselors, and other behavioral scientists, as well as laymen from a wide variety of backgrounds such as law, religion, and education. The organization publishes the *NARTH Bulletin* three times a year and archives back issues on its website. Also available online are reports, commentaries, interviews, testimonials, and a recommended reading list.

Parents, Families, and Friends of Lesbians and Gays (PFLAG)
PFLAG National Office
1828 L St. NW, Ste. 660
Washington, DC 20036
(202) 467-8180 • fax: (202) 349-0788
e-mail: info@pflag.org • website: http://community.pflag.org

PFLAG is a national organization that supports the health and well-being of gay, lesbian, bisexual, and transgender persons and their families and friends through support, education, and advocacy. The group maintains an online newsroom and also provides tools for creating safe schools, as well as a variety of reports on issues including marriage, hate crimes, workplace discrimination, and the "don't ask, don't tell" policy.

Rockford Institute
934 N. Main St.
Rockford, IL 61103
(815) 964-5053
e-mail: rkfdinst@bossnt.com

The Rockford Institute seeks to rebuild moral values and recover the traditional American family of a male and female parent with children. It believes that AIDS is a symptom of the decline of the traditional family, and it insists that only by supporting traditional families and moral behavior will America rid itself of the disease. The institute publishes the periodicals *Family in America* and the *Religion & Society Report* as well as various syndicated newspaper articles that occasionally deal with the topic of AIDS.

Servicemembers Legal Defense Network (SLDN)
PO Box 65301
Washington, DC 20035-5301
(202) 328-3244 or (202) 328-FAIR • fax: (202) 797-1635
e-mail: sldn@sldn.org • website: www.sldn.org

The SLDN is a national nonprofit legal service, watchdog, and policy organization dedicated to ending discrimination against and harassment of gay military personnel affected by the "don't ask, don't tell" policy. It provides free legal services to service members harmed by "don't ask, don't tell" and related discriminatory policies, and it advocates for policies and practices that improve the lives of service members. The group's website collects press releases and news stories and also publishes a blog and online forum called *The Frontline*.

BIBLIOGRAPHY

Books

M.V. Badgett, *When Gay People Get Married: What Really Happens When Societies Legalize Same-Sex Marriage*. New York: New York University Press, 2010.

Alan Chambers, *Leaving Homosexuality: A Practical Guide for Men and Women Looking for a Way Out*. Eugene, OR: Harvest House, 2009.

Michael Coogan, *God and Sex: What the Bible Really Says*. New York: Twelve, 2010.

Joe Dallas and Nancy Heche, *The Complete Christian Guide to Understanding Homosexuality: A Biblical and Compassionate Response to Same-Sex Attraction*. Eugene, OR: Harvest House, 2010.

Steve Estes, *Ask and Tell: Gay and Lesbian Veterans Speak Out*. Chapel Hill: University of North Carolina Press, 2008.

Fred Fejes, *Gay Rights and Moral Panic: The Origins of America's Debate on Homosexuality*. New York: Palgrave Macmillan, 2011.

Nathaniel Frank, *Unfriendly Fire: How the Gay Ban Undermines the Military and Weakens America*. New York: Thomas Dunne, 2009.

Evan Gerstmann, *Same-Sex Marriage and the Constitution*. New York: Cambridge University Press, 2008.

Janelle Hallman, *The Heart of Female Same-Sex Attraction: A Comprehensive Counseling Resource*. Downer's Grove, IL: InterVarsity, 2008.

Kelly Huegel, *GLBTQ: The Survival Guide for Gay, Lesbian, Bisexual, Transgender, and Questioning Teens*. Minneapolis: Free Spirit, 2011.

Paul Jackson, *One of the Boys: Homosexuality in the Military During World War II*. Montreal: McGill-Queen's University Press, 2010.

Jennifer Wright Knust, *Unprotected Texts: The Bible's Surprising Contradictions About Sex and Desire*. New York: HarperOne, 2011.

Bronson Lemer, *The Last Deployment: How a Gay, Hammer-Swinging Twentysomething Survived a Year in Iraq*. Madison: University of Wisconsin Press, 2011.

Simon LeVay, *Gay, Straight and the Reason Why: The Science of Sexual Orientation*. New York: Oxford University Press, 2011.

Erwin W. Lutzer, *The Truth About Same-Sex Marriage: Six Things You Must Know About What's Really at Stake*. Chicago: Moody, 2010.

Francis MacNutt, *Can Homosexuality Be Healed?* Grand Rapids, MI: Chosen, 2006.

Darren Main, *Hearts and Minds: Talking to Christians About Homosexuality*. Forres, Scotland: Findhorn, 2008.

National Defense Research Institute, *Sexual Orientation and U.S. Military Personnel Policy: An Update of RAND's 1993 Study*. Santa Monica, CA: Rand, November 30, 2010.

Frank Turek, *Correct, Not Politically Correct: How Same-Sex Marriage Hurts Everyone*. Charlotte, NC: CrossExamined, 2008.

Lynn D. Wardle, ed., *What's the Harm? Does Legalizing Same-Sex Marriage Really Harm Individuals, Families, or Society?* Lanham, MD: University Press of America, 2008.

Periodicals and Internet Sources

Jeff Amestoy, "Ultimate Battle for Gay Marriage Supporters: Their Fellow Americans," *Christian Science Monitor*, August 9, 2010.

David Blankenhorn, "Defining Marriage Down . . . Is No Way to Save It," *Weekly Standard*, April 2, 2007.

David Blankenhorn, "Protecting Marriage to Protect Children," *Los Angeles Times*, September 19, 2008.

Charles M. Blow, "Gay? Whatever, Dude," *New York Times*, June 5, 2010.

Tom Brannon, "What a Gay NCO Gave to the Marines," *Los Angeles Times*, December 25, 2010.

Daniel Burke, "Gay Debate Mirrors Church Split on Slavery," *National Catholic Reporter*, August 6, 2010.

Catholic Insight, "Catholic Schools Must Bar Teachers and Parents Involved in Homosexual Activism," April 2010.

Catholic Insight, "Cardinal Bertone, Pedophilia, Celibacy, and Homosexuality," May 2010.

Jason Cherkis, "Fear and Loathing: Can the Foster-Care System Deal with Gay Kids?," *Mother Jones*, November/December 2010.

Eve Conant, "Uncivil Rights?," *Newsweek*, December 14, 2010.

David France, "The Science of Gaydar," *New York*, June 25, 2007.

Mark Harris, "Too Gay? No Frickin' Way!," *Entertainment Weekly*, May 21, 2010. www.ew.com/ew/article/0,,20368911,00.html.

William F. Jasper, "Obama's 'Safe Schools Czar,'" *New American*, December 7, 2009.

Stanley Kurtz, "The Confession," *National Review Online*, October 31, 2006. www.nationalreview.com/articles/219092/confession/stanley-kurtz.

Jenny Lovell, "Living Outside the Liberal Bubble: Two Lesbian Moms Talk About Living in Conservative America," *Curve*, April 2010.

Julia McKinnell, "What to Do If Your Kid Says, 'I'm Gay,'" *Maclean's*, October 25, 2010. www2.macleans.ca/2010/10/19/what-to-do-gay.

Terrance McNally, "Perpetual Thoughts of Impurity," *Conscience*, Spring 2010.

Lisa Miller, "What the Bible Really Says About Sex," *Newsweek*, February 14, 2011.

Deroy Murdock, "Gay Marriage and Single Moms," *National Review Online*, March 19, 2009. www.nationalreview.com/corner/179027/gay-marriage-and-single-moms/deroy-murdock.

Matthew Parris, "The Gay Lobby Should Rejoice at the Pope's Argument That God Makes Us the Way We Are," *Spectator*, January 17, 2009. www.spectator.co.uk/columnists/all/3233616/another-voice.thtml.

Brian Powell, "Marriage and the Court of Public Opinion," *Los Angeles Times*, December 5, 2010.

Om Prakash, "The Efficacy of 'Don't Ask, Don't Tell,'" *Joint Force Quarterly*, no. 55, 4th quarter, 2009.

Frank Rich, "Two Weddings, a Divorce, and *Glee*," *New York Times*, June 13, 2010.

Bobby Ross, "Orphans on Deck: Adoption Steps to the Frontlines of the Culture Wars," *Christianity Today*, January 2010.

Sam Schulman, "Gay Marriage: Why Judge Walker Got Proposition 8 Wrong," *Christian Science Monitor*, August 6, 2010.

Jason Lee Steorts, "Two Views of Marriage and the Falsity of the Choice Between Them," *National Review Online*, February 7, 2011. www.nationalreview.com/articles/263672/two-views-marriage-jason-lee-steorts.

Jacob Sullum, "Strange Love: How I Learned to Stop Worrying and Embrace the Equal Protection Argument for Gay Marriage," *Reason*, November 2010.

Margaret Talbot, "Pride and Prejudice," *New Yorker*, October 25, 2010.

Pat Wingert with Barbara Kantrowitz, "What Makes a Family?," *Newsweek*, October 4, 2010.

Sara Eekhoff Zylstra, "Re-engineering Temptation: Fuzzy Science Sparks Debate over Treatments to Reverse Homosexuality," *Christianity Today*, May 2007.

A

American Psychological Association (APA), 31, 40, 42, 43

"Appropriate Therapeutic Responses to Sexual Orientation" (American Psychological Association), 43

B

Bailey, J. Michael, 22–23, 25

Bearman, Peter, 25

Besen, Wayne, 40

Bible
  condemnation of homosexuality by citing, is hypocritical, 16–19
  on lesbianism, 11–12
  says homosexuality is a sin, 10–15

Blankenhorn, David, 52–53, 57, 61

Brain
  changes in, correlate with homosexuality, 22, 27, 31
  prenatal impacts on, 29–30

Brückner, Hannah, 25

C

Chambers, Alan, 42

Civil unions, 63
  are a reasonable alternative to same-sex marriage, 61–66
  domestic partnerships, same-sex marriages and, state laws on, 72
  make homosexuals second-class citizens, 67–73
  should be allowed, 65
  states allowing, 72

Constitution, US. See First Amendment; Fourteenth Amendment

Cothran, Charlene, 42

Cott, Nancy, 56, 59

D

Defense of Marriage Act (1996), 64

Domestic partnerships, states allowing, 72

Don't ask, don't tell policy, 8
  assessment on impact of repeal of, 77
  repeal will have little effect on US military, 74–82
  should be repealed, 83–87

Due Process Clause, 54
marriage protected by, 54
Duncan, Robert, 16

E
Environment, homosexuality
results from a combination
of genetics and, 26–31
Equal protection clause
(Fourteenth Amendment),
8
Exodus International, 41,
42, 43

F
First Amendment, 62
Fourteenth Amendment,
8, 71

G
Gay marriage. *See* Same-sex
marriage
Gay rights, opposition to,
6–7
Genetics
homosexuality results
from a combination of
environment and, 26–31
sibling pairs/twins and, by
sex, *24*
studies showing link with
homosexuality are flawed,
22–25
twin studies and, 22–25,
24, 27–29, 30

Gordon, Gary, 7

H
Ham, Carter F., 74
Hamer, Don, 23
Heterosexual marriage
same-sex marriage does not
harm, 51–60
same-sex marriage would
undermine, 44–50
Homosexuality/homosexual
attractions
Bible says is a sin, 10–15
can be changed, 32–39
cannot be changed,
40–43
citing Bible to condemn, is
hypocritical, 16–19
is not inborn, 20–25
myths about, 22
results from a combination
of genes and environment,
26–31
Homosexual(s)
are not born gay, 20–25
discrepancy between
having gay sexual
experience and identifying
as, *35*

J
Jackson, Jesse, 8
Jeter, Mildred, 58
Johnson, Jeh Charles, 74
Jones, Mike, 40–41

L

Lawrence v. Texas (2003),
54
Lesbianism, Bible on,
11–12
LeVay, Simon, 22
Leviticus (book of Bible)
  condemnation of
    homosexuality in, 11,
    12, *12*
Loving, Richard, 58
Loving v. Virginia (1967),
  56, 59, 71

M

Marriage
  as fundamental right,
    71–73
  Supreme Court, US, views
    on, 8, 54, 55–56, 71
  See also heterosexual
    marriage; same-sex
    marriage
McAlvey, Patrick, 40–42
McCain, John, 83, 86
Meacham, Jon, 16
Military, US
  don't ask, don't tell policy
    and, 74–82, 83–87
  foreign, gays/lesbian in,
    82
  US, racial/gender
    integration of, 80–82
Miller, Lisa, 17

O

Obama, Barack, 64, 65, 81, 83
opinion polls. *See* surveys

P

Park, Jason, 32, *38*
Paul (apostle), 11–12
Perry v. Schwarzenegger (CA,
  2010), 51
Pillard, Richard C., 22–23
Polls. *See* surveys
Prejean, Carrie, 14–15
Proposition 8 (CA), 8, 17,
  51, 52, 56

R

Ratliff, Mike, 10
Rauch, Jonathan, 61
Reparative therapy
  American Psychological
    Association verdict on,
    40, 43
  can be effective, 32–39
  ex-gay therapists and,
    40–41, 42
  no evidence supports efficacy
    of, 40–43

S

Same-sex marriage, 7
  Americans are ambivalent
    about, 65
  civil unions are a reasonable
    alternative to, 61–66

does not harm
heterosexual marriage,
51–60
laws on, by state, *46*
legislative/judicial actions
regarding, *47*
religious case for
supporting, 17–19
should be allowed, 65
should not be legally
recognized, 65
states allowing, *72*
support for, by age group,
55
would undermine
institution of marriage,
44–50
Schwarzenegger, Perry v.
(CA, 2010), 51
Sexual attraction/
orientation
can be changed, 32–39
cannot be changed, 40–43
factors contributing to, *30*
religious beliefs and, *14*
same-sex, incidence in
members of sibling pairs,
24
Sharp, Douglas, 67
Snyder, Matthew, 5
Sprigg, Peter, 20
Stacey, Judith, 50
Stalin, Josef, 10, 11
Starr, Barry, 26

States, US
allowing civil unions/
same-sex marriage, *72*
laws on same-sex marriage
by, *46*
Supreme Court, US,
rulings on marriage, 54, 60
views on marriage, 8, 53,
55–56
Surveys
of evangelicals, on same-
sex legal unions, 64
of service members on
repeal of don't ask, don't
tell, 75–78
on support of civil unions/
same-sex marriage, 64, 65
on support of same-sex
marriage, by age group, *55*
of US combat troops on
gays serving in military,
85
on whether gay service
members would like their
orientation known, 79

T
Texas, Lawrence v. (2003),
54
Trotsky, Leon, 10–11
Twin studies
refute biological basis for
homosexuality, 24–25
suggest genetic component
to homosexuality, 28–29

U

US Constitution. *See* First
    Amendment; Fourteenth
    Amendment

V

Virginia, Loving v. (1967),
    56, 59, 71

W

Warren, Rick, 11
Westboro Baptist Church
    protesters, 5, 6
    views of, on
        homosexuality, 5–6
Witherspoon Institute,
    44